LADY DOROTHIE FEILDING AT WAR

LADY DOROTHIE FEILDING AT WAR

'Right at the Heart and Pulse of Things'

CHRISTINE M. CLULEY

AMBERLEY

First published 2024

Amberley Publishing
The Hill, Stroud
Gloucestershire, GL5 4EP

www.amberley-books.com

Copyright © Christine M. Cluley, 2024

The right of Christine M. Cluley to be
identified as the Author of this work has been
asserted in accordance with the Copyright,
Designs and Patents Act 1988.

ISBN 978 1 3981 2131 7 (hardback)
ISBN 978 1 3981 2132 4 (ebook)

British Library Cataloguing in Publication Data.
A catalogue record for this book is available
from the British Library.

1 2 3 4 5 6 7 8 9 10

Typesetting by SJmagic DESIGN SERVICES, India.
Printed in the UK.

CONTENTS

I

LIFE BEFORE THE GREAT WAR

Lady Dorothie Feilding always did the unexpected. She was born on 6 October 1889, one month early, by breech, to the great surprise of her mother, Cecilia, and no doubt of her father, Viscount Feilding, the future 9th Earl of Denbigh.

The Denbighs were one of England's great aristocratic families, their title obtained in 1620. Legend had it that the family was descended from the Hapsburgs, but in the nineteenth century that was shown to be a myth. With typical Feilding insouciance, the family called themselves 'The Perhapsburgs'.

With great social courage, Dorothie's grandfather, Rudolph, the 8th earl, and his first wife, Louisa, had converted to Catholicism. His father was horrified and threated to disinherit him, but when Louisa died in 1853 they were reconciled. Rudolph married secondly Mary Berkeley of Spetchley Park, Worcestershire, a Catholic family, whose ancestry went back

The Lord-in-Waiting's daughters getting snails for the king (Edward VII).

to the medieval Lords Berkeley. Rudolph and Mary were models of piety and charity to the poor and sick. Mary kept a 'cauldron of good substantial soup', which was always on the fire for handing out to the poor. Rudolph took Christian charity still further and dressed the sores on the feet of tramps with his own hands.

Rudolph succeeded as the 8th earl in 1865. He and his wife established the habits of piety, charity and faith that earned him the title of 'a model squire', visiting one or other of his tenants every Sunday afternoon and sometimes working on the farm himself. He and the countess encouraged the poor and needy to call at the house, where he would personally give them food and drink and, if necessary, deal with their health problems. Their reputation was well known amongst their contemporaries; Lady Londonderry said of them, 'I declare nothing on earth could ever make those Denbighs worldly! No vaccination would get it into them.' Another observer commented that their unworldliness seemed to come so naturally to them. The 8th earl's children, including Dorothie's father, were born into this charitable Catholic family and continued the traditions of faith and good works.

Dorothie's mother, Cecilia, came from a longer established Catholic family. She was the daughter of Charles Hugh Clifford (1819-1880), 8th Baron Clifford of Chudleigh and Count Clifford, and the Hon. Agnes Louisa Catherine Petre. Although little is known about her childhood, her future relationship with Dorothie suggests a loving, supportive and

Newnham Paddox, Warwickshire.

The Earl and Countess of Denbigh and their seven daughters, Dorothie seated on the balustrade.

Christian environment. Cecilia and Viscount Feilding were married in September 1884.

It was into this happy, affectionate and pious Catholic family that Dorothie was born and brought up. Her childhood covered the last decade of Queen's Victoria's reign, and her teenage years the reign of Edward VII. He died in the year she reached 21. These decades have been considered as a golden age and Dorothie's life to this point reflects this description. Of course, it was not golden for the vast majority of the British population – there was dissatisfaction throughout the country on many issues.

The working classes were in turmoil struggling with social problems such as poverty, food shortages, overcrowded dwellings, and disease that killed more than half the population before the age of fifty. There was political unrest, with strikes in the workforce that were stirred up by activists such as the Syndicalist movement, demanding equality between workers and managers. Women were seeking equality with the support of the Suffragette movement.

Those in the higher levels of society were protected by their wealth and background from many of the consequences of all this unrest. Moreover, the Denbighs had the added advantage of being one of the few families who were not affected by the Agricultural Depression that had started during the 1870s and brought many landowners to the verge of ruin.

Life at Newnham Paddox, the family home, was indeed golden and the family very happy. Dorothie had three brothers, whom she adored. Rudolph, who was always known as Rollo, or Tubby, was the eldest. Hugh, the middle son was called Hughie, and occasionally 'Neb'. The youngest was Henry, who was always known as Peter. Dorothie was the second of six sisters and the eldest Mary, known as Mollie or Moll, was her close companion during her early years. Next was Agnes, followed by Marjorie, known as Marjie. Dorothie loved all her sisters but one of her favourites was Clare, who was similar to Dorothie in temperament. She was nicknamed 'Squeaker' or 'Squeaks' because one of her brothers had once pulled her hair and she had squealed out loudly. Elizabeth (Bettie) and Victoria (Taffy) were the youngest of this contented family.

Dorothie's character and her distinctive style of writing developed very early; she was probably three or four when she wrote to her mother:

Yesterday I went a long way by my self on the bickell I went 4 times roun the wilderness with outh stoping ones and agane from the tempell to the limewil and rond the little fir tree up to the black fir tree up to the black gate I send you a lot of kisses and hugs.

From Dorothie

In addition to the family letters, photograph albums record a life of enjoyment and pleasure both at home and visiting friends in England and in Europe. One of Dorothie's mother's many interests was photography, and she took hundreds of photographs which, to add to her practical skills, she developed herself: an interest that Dorothie inherited. A selection was put in albums and mostly labelled by the countess and as a celebration of their twentieth wedding anniversary she gave her husband a photograph album that recorded the family life at home and on holiday. This album reveals a very relaxed attitude toward and a great love of all their children. They and their friends can be seen digging for worms at the edge of the lake (for the lord-in-waiting to give the king), swimming, rolling down the sloping lawns and playing all sorts of games, including cricket, where Dorothie is seen with bare feet in the slips. In the winter of 1900, making full use of the snow and developing her horsemanship skills, she is sitting in a sleigh pulled by a small pony. There are no formal poses – just children laughing, enjoying themselves and looking happy.

Although the Denbighs were Catholic, religious differences were no longer a bar to any professions or appointments as they would once have been. Dorothie's father held the position of Lord-in-Waiting to Queen Victoria and was frequently involved with duties at court and very close to the Queen. In 1900, he was to accompany her as a member of the entourage when she made a visit to Ireland. When the Queen died the following January, he knew he would be 'told to look after somebody' for the period of her funeral. He was appointed to look after the King of Portugal and until the funeral was over he did not see much of his family. The countess took Mollie, her eldest daughter, Dorothie and the dowager Lady Denbigh to watch the funeral procession from the Household Stand at Buckingham Palace.

Life at home followed the pattern of that in most great houses. The winters were devoted to hunting with the local pack, the Atherstone Hunt, of which the earl was often Master. With the possible exception of the countess, all the family hunted, especially Dorothie, who adored horses and from a very early age was renowned for her expertise. The summers were spent either entertaining at home or visiting family friends all over the British Isles.

The Denbighs took their faith seriously and continued the traditions of the 8th earl and his countess. First thing every morning everyone on the estate, including the servants, governess, and estate workers, gathered for Mass in the chapel. After that the family took breakfast, then continued their day. For the children, education followed the typical pattern of rich families. A governess was employed for all of them, but at the age of seven the boys were sent to The Oratory School in Edgbaston. The girls continued to be taught by the governess until all but Dorothie were sent to St Mary's Priory at Princethorpe as day pupils, riding there and back each day accompanied by a groom.

The registers, now deposited at Douai Abbey, record all the other girls and their dates of attendance, including those of Imelda (Mellins) Harding, aged 16, Rollo's future wife. It seems that Dorothie did not attend with her sisters, but the archives are silent on why she, of all the girls, did not ride over each weekday, something she would have loved. As Dorothie, Mollie and Imelda were almost inseparable it is frustrating and vexing not to know the reason.

Although her spelling was idiosyncratic, her understanding of English grammar was excellent; this was owing to Janet Clinkard, the children's governess, who told the countess in a letter that Dorothie had 'cheered my soul today by writing "The king made him appear" as an example of the factitive object instead of "the king made him a peer"'.

As in most aristocratic families, daughters were sent to finishing establishments on the continent to learn a foreign language and 'finish' their education. In 1904 Dorothie was fifteen. She and Mollie were sent to the Convent of the Assumption in Paris and Dorothie's first letter home clearly expresses her practical common sense, and her firm opinions:

Dear Mother and Father
Thanks awfully for your P.C. We had a rather rough crossing but Ms & Miss Martin are very nice. We are going to them next Wednesday for tea, I think.

The two things we miss most after you are fresh air & animals. LSt night when we went into our bed-room the hot-air was turned on full – the window shuters & blinds & curtains tight shut, the consequence was that the air was rolling round the room in big lumps about the size of an orange – Animals consist off – not a bad but very mangy (to me!!) – dog & and some dirty hens. The dog is behind a grating & one can't get at it. The whole convent is simply boiling not so much with heat but thick undulated fug, & dozens of hot air things Ugh. They complain of being cold & walk about with shawls & cold. We have resolved to gain a 'Fresh Air' fund. Of course all the windows in this room are tight shut.

The madlle who brought us from the station is taken ill in bed to-day because – we insisted on opening the sash window at the top when it was running with fug!!!!!! (made in France)…

We were called at nine this morning & they gave us till 12 to get things straight. We got them to let us unpack ourselves so we made our list alright.

One of the day students became Dorothie's lifelong friend. She was Suzanne Hély d'Oissel, the daughter of General Hély d'Oissel, whom Dorothie met again in 1914 when she joined the Munro Ambulance Corps. Suzanne's daughter knew Dorothie and loved hearing stories from her mother about their time at the convent. Apart from the lack of fresh air there was another thing Dorothie did not understand – why they had to wash and bathe whilst keeping a long white shirt over their bodies. She asked the nun who was present, 'Why should we hide under these shirts? We are all women. Ce n'est pas si grave d'être nues entre nous!' The nun answered: 'The trouble is that we are not certain what sex are your Guardian Angels!'

Dorothie and Suzanne enjoyed their life and were quite mischievous but with no malice or spite. They often played jokes on one another. One evening Dorothie put several poissons rouges (goldfish) in Suzanne's bed. Other games were to see who could spit further and who could lift her leg higher up against a wall.

One of Dorothie's granddaughters attended the convent in the 1950s. One morning she was standing in the entrance hall with other pupils waiting to go into Mass. There was a winding staircase going up to the top of the building with bannisters from top to bottom. An old nun called her over. Had she been told about her grandmother and the stairs? She had not and was very amused to be told that when Dorothie was at the convent she always arrived just in time for lessons or outings but at the very last minute, breathless and smiling. On one particular day the scene was the same – pupils waiting quietly to go into Mass and no Dorothie. The nun called her name and from the top of the house came a voice: 'I'm coming'. They waited as Dorothie slid from top to bottom, cornering with perfect balance, landing with no mishap, a bright smile, and 'Ici, ici'. They all walked into Mass and nothing was said. Her horse-riding skills had certainly paid off.

Dorothie and Suzanne spent many holidays together at the Quesney in Normandy or at La Bussière, near Dijon in Burgundy. This property belonged to Suzanne's aunt, the Marquise de Ségur, and here she first met the Hély d'Oissel family and felt comfortable enough with them to call Suzanne's father 'Old Roger'.

On her return, life for Dorothie during the summers continued to be an enjoyable social round. In May 1908, Dorothie and her elder sister Mollie were presented at Court. However, her education was not yet complete. The countess arranged for Mollie and Dorothie to attend a Franciscan Convent at Taunton to take a course on domestic science and home management.

Imelda Harding and two of Dorothie's cousins also joined them. Her letters show all the wit and sense of fun that were to reappear in her wartime correspondence, alongside occasional thoughtlessness and expressions of frustration. Her ability to tell a story and to sum up a situation are also emerging, combined with her characteristic spelling and punctuation.

To her father:

> There is one old servant here who does odd jobs, & she can't get hold of our names at all, at all. The consequence is she calls us all wrong in the morning. If Angela is put down for 6 & Moll 7 o'clock she promptly reverses it & wakes an irate Moll an hour too early. The triumph was when she said to Gwenda the other day, 'Oh! I thought I was talking to Lady Mollie, but I see it is Miss Harding!!' One morning she annoyed me considerably by waking me up in the small hours to ask me if I was to know if she was to call me then or not! Altogether she is very original & I am afraid like Rollos summing up of Burcher whose family says 'cant of had any common sense among them for generations.'

To her sister Marjie:

> Also we are very lucky in the mistress as the head nun is a perfect dear. We have listened to them all 1) Winnie alias Sister Mary Win which is a fearful mouthfull she is the nice one. 2. 'Spoons' S. Antonia, this called because before we knew her name she taught us to clean spoons. She is a beastly nuisance always fussing & nosing around. Luckily we don't see much of her. 3 'Miss Peree' known as Peerie who is always here.

4) 'Bristles' who teaches us paper patterns. She will kiss us & is so beastly prickly to kiss! Also known as 'Gums' as she has not got a tooth in her head.

5) Mother Liquorice, so known because her name Mother Vicaress is so like it & because she reminds you of liquorice powder.

Today we ironed. Great amusement because I tried & succeeded in photographing Winnie! It was awfully funny. Hiding my camera behind my back I enticed her out into the drying yard in the sun on pretext of looking at a thing hanging up. Then we all called 'sister' & she turned round & I snapped her at 6 ft! We simply screamed & I rushed back into the house. It was awfully funny to watch her surprise as they are not allowed to be photographed. She quite saw the joke however & we teased her a lot about it ...

7.30 7.30 We get up according to if we are cooks etc. breakfast which we cook ourselves.

8.30 – 9 Mass

9 – 9.30 Dust & clean our rooms. Sat. spring clean

9.30 – 12.20 Go about our respective house duties, lunch cooked by the two cooks

11- 12 (I forgot to say we dressmake)

1.30 to 2 We learn alternate days cut paper patterns & sew

2–4 Free time. We go our (Saturdays free from lunchtime & Sundays we do nuffink sect our rooms

4- 5 tea & benediction

5.30 to 6 Nursing first aid lessons & sometimes accounts

6 to 7 We four (not cooks) go & cook dinner

7 Dinner then free to bed-time

Love from Diddles

Dorothie's letters sparkle with life and enjoyment – witty and pithy – and everything is so sharply observed. The lessons and skills learned from these two months of housekeeping were invaluable during her years in Flanders and in her married life. She was no doubt grateful for having such a sensible and far-sighted mother who encouraged all her daughters to be proficient in housekeeping, capable in all practical matters and to have confidence in their own judgement. The countess also made sure that each of her daughters had her own personal bank account, thus assuring her financial independence.

After these eight weeks of domestic tuition life continued as before. In most aristocratic and upper-class families one of the main purposes of the endless round of visits was to find suitable matches for their children, with many families insisting on marriages based on financial gain, or social climbing, the partner often chosen by the parents. The Feildings were much more lenient. One reason may have been that they had no financial pressures to consider. The only restriction was that they had to marry Catholics and other than this, the earl and countess did not force any of their children to marry against their will. The first one to marry was Rollo, who married Mellins. Her stepmother was a sister of the countess and Mellins had stayed at Newham Paddox since she was a child, attending school with Dorothie and Mollie. Dorothie's sisters, Mollie and Marjie, met their prospective husbands on family visits and married within a few weeks of one another in 1915, and even though Mollie was 26 when she married, she had known her future husband a long time.

In the years leading up to the war Dorothie had not found a suitable husband from this small circle of eligible young men. However, in a letter written in 1917 Dorothie reminded her mother of the friendship she once had with Thomas Fitzherbert Brockholes, the second son of an old established Catholic family from Lancashire. They were close friends of the Feildings and Dorothie explained that it was sometime before the war that she started to think a great deal of him. He had joined the 3rd Battalion Rifle Brigade 1908 but in July 1910 transferred to the 2nd Battalion and went to Calcutta. Dorothie did not see him during the next four years, but they wrote to each other and began to grow closer and feel a great affection for each other. They had not become engaged, but Dorothie was convinced they would have done when they next met and they both thought it would have been quite soon. However, he did not come back until the outbreak of war and within three weeks transferred to the Western Front, giving them no time to meet again and consolidate their feelings.

Dorothie believed that Tom was the man she would marry and being high principled and loyal she treated all other men as she would her brothers, as friends and 'pals'. Tall, beautiful, elegant, always perfectly dressed, and with an infectious sense of humour, Dorothie's personality made her a very popular companion. Nevertheless, her behaviour did not reflect the typical image and style required of Victorian and Edwardian young women. She was very close to her sister Mollie, who was known to be 'very proper' and never acted or made a decision without a great deal of thought, and her friend and future sister-in-law, Mellins, who was very petite and feminine. Both were the epitome of perfect young ladies, unlike Dorothie, who could have been described as a tomboy, robust and spirited, bursting with boundless energy and with a love of outdoor pursuits (taking risks on some occasions that caused her family some concern). Although she loved her sisters and her female friends, she felt more comfortable with and preferred the company of men, with whom she felt completely at ease. All through her wartime experiences it was the men who were her companions and sought her company. She wrote to her mother in May 1915: 'Here am I out here, wearing trousers & hoping people will look on me like a boy just because I feel & look like one.' Most of all, she adored her brothers and they in their turn adored her.

Whilst waiting for Tom's return, life continued as usual for Dorothie and her family until June 1914, when the assassination of Archduke Ferdinand and his wife in Sarajevo led to the greatest upheaval of the modern world and changed the life of the Denbighs and millions of others forever. Country after country in Europe was drawn into the war. When Germany invaded Belgium, contravening the Treaty of London of 1839, Britain was forced to declare war.

Even before the start of hostilities five members of Dorothie's family were already in uniform. The earl was a reserve colonel in the Royal Artillery. Rudolf (Rollo), his eldest son, served as a lieutenant in the Coldstream Guards; Hugh was a lieutenant commander in the navy; Peter (Henry) was training in the reserve cavalry regiment of King Edward's Horse, later transferring to the Coldstream Guards. Men were obviously needed in their military capacity but there was a huge call for help in many other ways, and this was where women were able to volunteer and provide essential services.

As the German invasions continued and reports of deaths and casualties began to appear in the newspapers, Dorothie was determined to do something useful. Her uncle, Everard Feilding, was attached to the War Office and had established a committee in London to provide the armies in Flanders with extra ambulances and volunteers. He suggested one for Dorothie – The Munro Ambulance Corps.

Dr Hector Munro had advertised for adventurous young women to staff an ambulance unit for service in Belgium and Dorothie was one of 200 applicants, from whom he accepted only four. Dorothie was adventurous, could drive and spoke excellent French; however, she lacked nursing experience, so she immediately applied for and was taken on to a three-week 'crash course' in nursing at the Hospital of St Cross in Rugby to prepare her for work with the injured soldiers. On 10 September, 'sitting on the sink' she explained to her father:

> I get twenty minutes off for meals & most of that time is spent chewing the cud & not much of it left for correspondence – But one gets two hours off somewhere in the day – I like being here awfully – Tho I must say its pretty hard work as you dont get off your flat feet from 6 a.m. to 10 p.m. & what with 'nurse I want to be sick' etc you are kept on the move – But the nurses are all very nice & dont a bit mind showing & explaining one things – I felt terribly clumsy the first days, but am much more use now.
>
> [24 August 1914]

She confided in her mother that she was impatient with herself, she was 'getting on well here but wish one didn't take so long getting a grasp on new things – It's a bit depressing sometimes but I s'pose no one yet learnt a lot about anything in a week.' However, she was to gain very high marks when she completed the course.

On 22 September, having finished her three-week training and being in possession of her nursing certificate, she and her mother visited Dr Munro to finalise the details. Hector Munro had plans to work in Flanders. His qualifications were impressive: MB, CM (Bachelor of Medicine, Master of Surgery, Aberdeen University). He had been born in Glasgow in 1869, had served as a ship's doctor and had studied psychology with Freud in Vienna. In 1913 he had started a psychiatric hospital in London, the Medico-Psychological Clinic, but now he saw an opportunity to be useful in the war effort in Belgium. Dorothie soon summed him up as a scatterbrain and a dreamer.

He was sitting on the floor playing with a shiny new canvas green tent of complicated designs. No kind of use, and surrounded by maps. Between the intervals of showing us how it buttoned up and where Ghent was we gradually discovered the expedition was a motley gathering varying in number from (he wasnt quite sure which) of people calculated to be of any use at all at the front – We had two cars, where no one seemed to know and we hoped that they were at Ostend – Our destinations were Ghent which sometimes had Uhlans [mounted German cavalry] and sometimes hasnt any wounded motor ambulances – There were none – We had collected £40 by writing to the papers and deposited it with McConnell who next day left in a hurry for America with the result that the money was hung up and quite ungettable – We were to bring passports and meet at Victoria the next day.

May Sinclair was the only other person there and told me with ardour not to mind the Munro vagueness as he was a Celtic poet and dreamer and had magnificent ideals. I didn't see dreams were going to finance the corps or ideals get us to Ghent but I left it at that and hoped for the best. Father had given me enough money to get home with if I didnt like it and as I was not more than an average fool and capable of looking after myself. I got inoculated & prepared to leave. By the way Munro inoculated me – he held the syringe upside down & dropped the serum. He wondered how much he should put in if he didnt get the right dose. He forgot to boil any of the instruments – I concluded his Doctor lore would not carry him very far.

Her mother accompanied her to London and saw her daughter undertake the first stage of her journey to the Western Front. All Dorothie's practical skills in domestic management, gardening, and self-discipline, acquired both at home and at school, and her excellent French, would be extremely useful during the next three years. Her aristocratic rank gave her the confidence to deal with those of her level with respect but not awe, and those of the lower social level with kindness and patience. Added to this was her deep love for her family, her happy home life and her deep, unquestioning religious faith and honesty. Most of all, her exceptional skills in writing portrayed a very personal and close-up view of the war from all perspectives: tragic and funny, heroic and cowardly, strong support but blind stupidity, great generosity and desperate need. These letters, vibrant, amusing, and brilliantly descriptive, bring to life how the Great War was fought out in one corner of Europe.

I arrived at Victoria with too much luggage. The wrong kind of clothes (not rough enough) a raging temperature and a black eye & awful feeling of homesickness. I had a feeling in my bones that fun and unusual things were going to happen and that risks would come my way. Mother, owing to our starting late had arranged to go to another member of the family. But no one showed any interest or concern in my departure & I didnt like to suggest it but Edie came to see me off so I blessed her for it.

The most weird crowd collected at that train & I kept wondering which of them belonged to our party & hoping the ladies in huge coats and hats at the bookstall and the cadaverous gent in the pepper & salt suit, and the fat man in khaki, and the little American lady, with a twang did not belong to us. But they did! And they hoped the girl with a bloodshot eye & multi-coloured face was not coming – but she was!

[23 September 1914]

Dorothie did not mention that amongst her 'too much luggage' was her pet dog.

2

GETTING THE SHOW ON THE ROAD

By the time that Dorothie arrived in Belgium the war had been underway for nearly two months. Germany had declared war on Russia on 1 August and demanded that France remain neutral, but France had mobilized on the same day. The first French soldier had been killed the day after, although the official declaration of war by Germany on France was not made until 3 August.

In order to advance into France, the Germans asked the Belgians for permission to cross their country, but neutral Belgium rejected Germany's request. Germany then declared war on Belgium. Britain, Belgium's ally, was therefore obliged to declare war on Germany. Despite strong resistance by the allied forces, the Germans made significant advances through Belgium causing the British Expeditionary Force (BEF) to retreat from Mons in August. But the allied armies counter-attacked in the First Battle of the Marne in early September

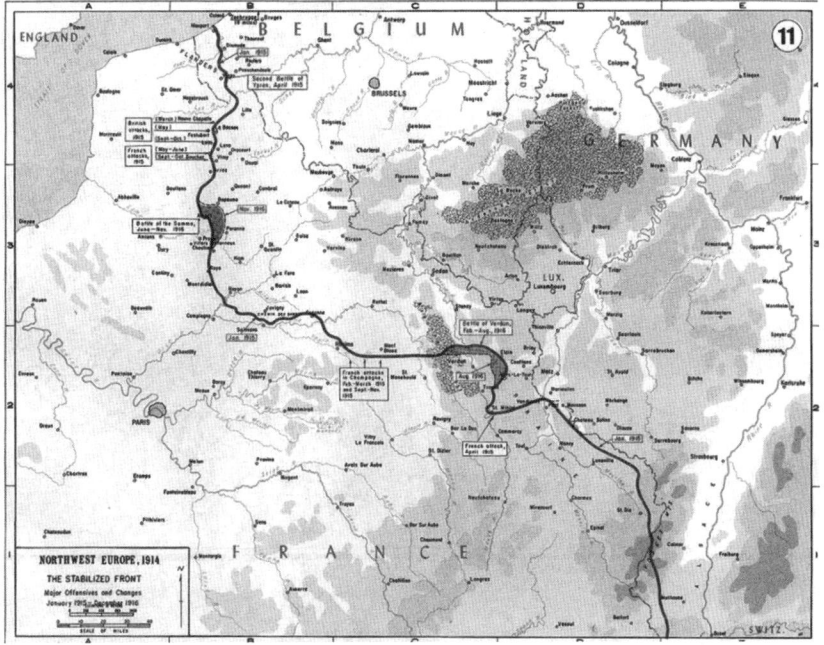

Northwest Europe, 1914 – the stabilized Front.

and the German advance was brought to a halt within 30 miles of Paris. Four years of trench warfare ensued.

On 25 September, Dorothie set off on her great adventure and from the first day she began her letters home, filling them with details and opinions to keep her family informed and lessen their anxiety about her. On the train to Folkestone, she explained that she was feeling much better as her typhoid injection had now worn off, but she also made a joking allusion to an act of contrition she had made before starting the journey. She had 'made my soul with a dirty pig of a German padre at Farm Street [London] ... who was furious at being asked for when I hadn't even a mortal sin for him. He was such a pig I nearly turned mahomadan on the spot.'

Although the tone may be reassuring and humorous, religion was always a serious matter to Dorothie. She never doubted her belief in God and was firm in her Catholic faith, putting trust in God's purposes.

She could still, though, feel the loss of family friends – 'It's awful reading about Brigham & others who have since gone' – but she continued to reassure her mother that Rollo, her elder brother, 'will come home to us all right'. She finished the letter with her usual breezy assurances: 'God bless you all & don't worry about me. I'll turn up all right & if I find one is useless there or things turn out badly run I can so easily come home with my funds.'

Dorothie of course knew her mother would be concerned for the four of her children who were involved in the war. Other men closely associated with the family were also in uniform, including Edward Dudley Hanly (known to the family as Dudley), the fiancé of Dorothie's sister Marjie. Anxious to be near him, Marjie also trained as a nurse and had gone to a hospital in Dunkirk. Dorothie's letters home always contained words of reassurance to her concerned mother.

I have been thinking so much of you all yesterday & today, it must be like dragging off a large piece of your heart to see Rollo go, but I am so glad you had time to go down there – I know & feel God will bring him safe back again & it is so splendid to feel one can be proud of them wanting to go off isn't it? But its awful for the poor mothers – This awful war just swallows up everyone's happiness in the most limitless way, & I have been aching for you for what you have been going through.

[22 September 1914]

And this was only eight weeks into the war. Dorothie provided the countess with a very clear description of her fellow corps members:

We are a dozen going today. 4 women, 4 doctors, 1 Red Cross parson & 2 motor men owners & mechanics – Mrs Knocker, the leading lady & trained nurse, A1 thank God, inspires me with great confidence & seems most capable. I was very relieved to find someone of that kind of stuff in this contingent as I was rather doubting the capabilities of Miss Sinclair – but it's Mrs Knocker I see will run the show Dr Head ... told me about Munro ... he was thoroughly trustworthy & a good sort & I would be quite OK with him. The only fault he had was vagueness & told me to follow my own judgement in matters of prudence & initiative ... But if I did, that would be all right ... Miss Chisolm a strong buxom colonial pal of [Elsie Knocker] & capable, an American lady hanger on & quite useless thou' much obliging, Miss Sinclair ditto, two young doctors – sports & good souls & will get a move on, A Mr Gurney an engineer & car mechanic – not a gentleman but a good soul & knows his job. Then a boy scout parson about 35 (not a child) a well meaning ass.

The women had already been noted by Philip Gibbs, war reporter for the *London Daily Chronicle*. He described them as strikingly beautiful people:

I had met some of the party in Malo-les-Bains, where they had reassembled before coming to Furnes, and I had been puzzled by them. In the 'flying column', as they called their convoy of ambulances, were several ladies very practically dressed in khaki coats and breeches, and very girlish in appearance and manners. They did not seem to me at first sight the type of women to be useful on a battlefield or in a field-hospital. I should have expected them to faint at the sight of blood, and to swoon at the bursting of a shell. Some of them at least were too pretty, I thought, to play about in fields of war among men and horses smashed to pulp.

[Philip Gibbs, *The Soul of War.* 1915
pp.176-71]

Gibbs mirrored the prevailing British opinion on the rôle of women at a time of war. Women in uniform crossed the boundary between the sexes. Military uniforms were the privilege of the men, as was the right to defend the country and the women in it. The rôle of women was to be defended, and they should be prevented by all means from going to the front as Amazons in khaki. The women he was describing proved him to be wrong. Again and again, they showed that they were useful in both battlefield and hospital, and none of them swooned or fainted at the sight of blood or the bursting of a shell.

In addition to Dorothie, the second woman in the corps was Elizabeth 'Elsie' Knocker. From a middle-class background, she had been adopted as a young child by Lewis Upcott, a schoolmaster at Marlborough, and his wife. In 1906 she had married Leslie Duke Knocker and a son was born the next year. The marriage failed and they were divorced, but she kept this secret as female divorcées were socially unacceptable in Edwardian England. She let it be known that she was a widow, and the truth was not revealed for several years. Elsie was a woman with an unusual amount of vigour and ambition. She had independent means that allowed her to enjoy her interest in riding motorcycles and she became a member of The Gypsy Motorcycle Club and took part enthusiastically in its trials. She also spoke French, which was a great advantage for service at the front.

The third member, Mairi Chisholm, was the daughter of a Scottish landowner and another motorcycle enthusiast. She was only eighteen but, despite her youth and upper-class background, she was experienced with auto mechanics and motorcycles. She was also a member of the Gypsy Motorcycle Club where she met Elsie. After the British declaration of war, Elsie suggested they went to London to become despatch riders in the Women's Emergency Corps. Hector Munro spotted Mairi hurtling through the London streets and, stopping her, invited her to join his Corps. She agreed on condition that her friend Elsie could also join.

The fourth female member of Munro's corps, Helen Hayes, was an American music teacher. She was married and her husband, Arthur Gleason, a renowned left-wing journalist and a proponent of American entry into the war, was active as a war reporter in Belgium. He asked a famous war writer,

… whose breast was gay with the ribbons of half a dozen campaigns, what was the matter with all these women, that they did not tremble and go green under fire, as some of us did. He said: 'They don't belong out here. They have no business to be under fire. They ought to be back at the hospitals down at Dunkirk. They don't appreciate danger. That's the trouble with them; they have no imagination.'

Had Dorothie been aware of this comment it would have elicited a very sharp riposte! Gradually, however, public opinion altered, and Gibbs changed his mind. With so many men being killed, there were no longer enough left both to fight and to service the war effort and women were required to take on some of these duties. Women rose to the challenge and proved that they could make an invaluable contribution. 'It was only later that I saw their usefulness and marvelled at the spiritual courage of these young women, who seemed not only careless of shell-fire but almost unconscious of its menace, and who, with more nervous strength than that of many men, gave first-aid to the wounded without shuddering at sights of agony which might turn a strong man sick.' (*The Soul of War* p.177.)

Gibbs may have learned to respect these women but there was one member of the corps whose competence Dorothie never credited. This was the renowned English authoress May Sinclair, whom Dorothie described as an ass on several occasions. She was responsible for the book-keeping, maintaining daily records and writing for the newspapers to generate money for the operation of the ambulance unit, because they were all unpaid volunteers who had to bear the costs for their own equipment. Whatever her book-keeping skills, May Sinclair was a little too prone to panic for Dorothie's taste.

Courage would certainly be required as the war gained pace around Dorothie and her comrades. Part of the German war plan was to isolate Antwerp to counter the possibility that Belgian forces, reinforced by British troops, would threaten the northern flank of the German armies involved in the invasion of France. Aware of this, the Belgian army had been ordered to retreat to Antwerp and had arrived on 20 August.

The Germans continued their advance and bombarded the town on 28 September. Early the next day, the Belgian Prime Minister, Charles de Broqueville, informed the British that if all the outer forts were lost, the government and field army of 65,000 men would withdraw to Ostend and leave the 80,000 fortress troops to hold Antwerp for as long as possible. De Broqueville then formally appealed to the British and French governments for help and preparations to evacuate the Belgian army to Ostend were begun. The wounded, recruits, untrained men, prisoners of war, transport, equipment, ammunition, and industrial machinery were gradually moved from Antwerp.

The BEF had just reached the River Aisne at Picardy, Northern France, as the ambulance corps arrived in Ostend at

A German celebration of General von Beseler's triumph.
'Antwerp, The King of the Scheld River/Your country is in pieces,/Because of German Swords./Now we can tell everyone/About you the King./The Germans have liberated you,/Taken you over by force,/That was like a wedding/ Accompanied by thunder and lightning.'

7 pm on Friday 25 September. Ostend was full of refugees from Louvain, Antwerp, Termonde, Alost and Brussels, as well as conscript troops getting to the station of Ostend or to the local barracks. Some of them found a place to stay in a few hundred white bathing carts rolled together in neat rows behind the Royal Galleries. Dorothie described a great flutter in the town because a zeppelin had dropped five bombs. This was the first close experience of the war. Dorothie acerbically commented that 'Miss Sinclair who may be brainy but is a perfect ass on this kind of expedish, (& who the devil wants a sec. anyway?) was in a panic & said it wasn't safe, & the Germans would come again & being in the Station Hotel & they trying for the station etc. etc. etc. – But we had a very peaceful night.'

Dorothie's Uncle Everard (Evy) helped establish a committee in London to provide the corps in Flanders with extra ambulances and volunteers. In early November, four additional ambulances and eleven new volunteers would turn up in Furnes to join the original corps, but at this moment there was 'all sorts of trouble the next day because unable get petrol without endless formalities thro' the militaries ... Hope to get off soon though & muddle through in the true British way & once in Ghent we will be quite all right'. The fuel had all been requisitioned by the Belgian army. However, Dorothie's perfect French soon resolved the problem and the Red Cross president from Ghent met the Corps and made arrangements for them to be put up free in Ghent. They were given two 'vast motor ambulances, old pattern Daimler & Fiat & two chauffeurs & a light Ford to follow us today. Saw some Red X people tho' from Antwerp today who say they have 11,000 beds prepared & no wounded & nothing on earth for

Mrs Stobart's people to do. So I'm jolly glad we didn't go with them and are much more likely to be useful.' She described the scene in Ostend as being most peaceful '& not a bit war-like. The sea full of submarines yesterday. Looked chilly work – poor beggars. Anchored just on watch like that'.

Always aware of her family's concerns about her safety she tells then not to worry: 'No kind of danger – These Red X men we met here have been doing our work for 6 weeks & told us a lot about it – you aren't allowed any where near the actual fighting line & there are not Germans at Ghent tho' they can come if they want – It's not under German as I imagined which is splendid.'

Finally, having sorted out their problems, they set off on the road to Ghent via Bruges and Eeklo in the opposite direction to the increasing flow of refugees. They were told that German Uhlans had been exploring the area of Ghent but had made no attempt to enter the city. Dorothie and the corps arrived on 27 September and found Ghent entirely under Belgian control and 'in no kind of danger', although she was aware that as an unfortified town anyone could enter, friend or foe. She quickly assessed that the Belgian ladies who were running the hospital were 'thundering good too for amateurs – organisation A1 & beat English Red X into fits'.

Their first impression of the town was a happy one. They were met by a huge crowd of 'Ghentites' who she said loved them on the spot because they were English and made them very welcome. Also, the hotel was comfortable and there was 'no sort of roughing'. She found it hard to believe that a war was going on, although they were aware of skirmishes occurring all the time between twelve and thirty miles away and saw eight or nine wounded brought in. Eager to get going, she was exasperated by the endless red tape about passports which prevented the corps from doing anything and she 'had begun to think the war would be over before we got a job' when one of the ambulances was called up in the middle of lunch and went off with two of the doctors. Action at last!

Military Hospital No. 2 had taken over the chic Hotel Flandria next to the railway station in Ghent. Its revolving doors had been removed and the Persian rugs rolled up. The only guests now were about a hundred wounded Belgian and German soldiers. A week later, there were 300 more, and shortly after another 500. There were also British wounded among them, hastily evacuated by train from besieged Antwerp. Ghent by now was overrun by refugees and the

Hotel Flandria today, Brussels.

Munro Corps helped with food distribution at the Festival Palace in the Citadel Park. Dorothie recorded that they 'fed 6,000 2 days ago from noon to 4.30 – poor beggars'.

Dorothie was highly critical of how the corps was being managed and was pleased that another doctor, Dr Renton, had joined the party that day. 'Jolly glad too he's a good man & we badly need "heads" to organise this party which is sadly sloppy – But we are trying to kick ourselves into shape & get things going.' No doubt much of the 'kicking' was encouraged by Dorothie.

After the initial excitement things slowed down and Dorothie was desperate for action and critical of the lack of organisation:

Oh the awful inactivity of the 1st few days in Ghent – We felt if we were not up to our eyes in work all day & all night that we were there on false pretences – And there was nothing to do in the hospital and very little to do on the cars & there was no need for 14 people per car & if anyone went it should be the doctors and what was the use of being a woman anyway?

Marie [Mairi] and I sat forlornly in the square & wishing we were dead – Wishing we had the moral courage to go home and own to failure – Wishing something would happen and aching for work – All we did up Ghent way could have been done by one third of the number and all the time one was not helping – one felt the ridiculousness of those numbers crowded on the cars – But anyway I was a help by my French – no one knew a word hardly except for Mrs Knocker & I had to run around – get passports – badger the Colonels & the Belgian army in general for permission to go where there was wounded – Find

Munro, lose him again & find him again – tell him he was a
mess & why couldn't he keep appointments with officials – but
he couldn't & never will. It is just beyond his power. All those
ways I could help & did help & ended by getting the show a lot
nearer things than they would otherwise.

[Diary September 1915]

Having got the show on the road, Dorothie at last found
out what the job involved. On 28 September she completed
her first job on the ambulance and reported being very well
and happy and for the first time got near the battlefields at
Dendermonde and Termond. The ambulance was to go
between three to five miles from the firing line, or as near as
the military authorities would let them, pick up the wounded
who were brought to them by orderlies and take them to a
dressing station and then, if necessary, the hospital. There was
very little medical work done on the field – just iodine and a
dry dressing and 'all dirt left on for luck'.

Frightfully exciting & we brought back five wounded. One, a
German shot thro' the head who won't recover we are afraid poor
devil – It's most impressive being outside there & seeing all the
troops & being in the midst of things – It's hard to realise the war
in the town itself tho' all this happens a few miles out – Perpetual
skirmishes & dribbles of wounded all the time – Everyone here is
mad over us & England & we have the time of our lives.

[28 September 1915]

The shock of war and its carnage had not yet affected
Dorothie and the capture of a German car amused her. It had

been ambushed by two Belgian officers whose five 'A1' shots through the radiator and the wounding of both Germans she described as 'great fun'. The car was covered with 'pots of gore – the screen bashed to smithereens & we amused ourselves picking bullets out of the bodywork'.

She was more bothered about Miss Sinclair who was in a fuss because she believed Lady Denbigh had made her responsible for Dorothie's welfare. Dorothie quickly disabused her of this belief and told her that she had taken all responsibility for herself. In Dorothie's opinion Miss Sinclair was utterly useless at practical things. 'Thank God I can look after myself & am now under Mrs Knocker's jurisdiction – She is a capable woman & fit to give orders & I am safe as houses with her.'

By 2 October there was nothing much doing as the fighting had stopped nearly everywhere and Dorothie was critical of the descriptions in the newspaper of the fighting at Alost, which she said were much exaggerated: 'We were thereabouts so know'. However, in the next few days Dorothie explained that she had precious little time for letter writing as they had been very busy helping to bring in wounded – 300 one night and 500 the next – from the train. She saw trainloads of British tommies going in the opposite direction and commented, 'It's rather awful to see the two trains meet & thinking how little the reinforcements know what they are in for.' She was also disgusted by the military doctor who was in overall commend of them. He 'suffers from severe funk & won't let us really get hold of people that otherwise just die in the trenches for want of being fetched'.

Dorothie would have made a very efficient war reporter. She missed very little; she noted the heavy skirmishing and shelling round Termonde and was aware that the Germans were trying to build pontoon bridges over the Scheldt there, despite 'the Belgians lining the river putting a spoke in their wheel'. Dorothie's fearlessness was to become well-known, but it occasionally caused problems. When they arrived at 'where the guns were popping, the old Belgian doctor got such a funk he just threw himself out of our bus & refused to go on, so we blew kisses to him & left.' No doubt this swift departure was instigated by Dorothie. They went right up to the trenches and took back some badly wounded men, walking three miles each way, carrying the stretchers, taking cover when necessary and walking over slippery banks. It was 8.30 pm when they got to the ambulance as they had lost their way in the dark and the ambulance could not show its lights. 'Those poor beggars had been lying there since 8am this morning & would have died if they had had the night out as well, which would have been the case if it hadn't been for us.'

Unfortunately, their courageous actions were not admired or seen as resourceful.

Our doctor funk pal we had thrown out went to the military authorities & said we had disobeyed his orders & in fact raised Hell generally & today we have been put right back & not allowed to go anywhere near anything & that is what happens every time we try & break out a bit & try to do what is really needed. Because at present the military won't send their ambulances nearer then 5 kms to the firing line, which means that men are just dying there, as Rollo says, for want of immediate help & because the doctors just funk it – so now we arrange a new scheme.

[7 October 1914]

Their alternative plan, which they put in place the next day, was for the men to procure light cars and obtain passes to get to where the wounded were and then bring them back to where the women were waiting with the two ambulances, thus overcoming the problem of the women not being allowed near the front. The wounded were transferred to the ambulances and brought to the hospital in Ghent. In that way they got to the surgeons more quickly, increasing their chances of survival. But the ambulance work was becoming more dangerous and always shocking. As they waded through a turnip field at Kwatrecht looking for survivors, Mairi Chisholm shuddered at what she saw; 'I have never in my life seen so much blood. Lying in and out among the turnips were dead and dying Germans – all looked like figures out [of] wax – their fingers sticking out straight and rigid.' (Undated typescript letter, National Library Scotland.)

By 5 October, Dorothie was reporting disheartening news from Antwerp, where the fortresses were being defended against the Germans by Belgian troops supported by three British naval brigades. She noted that some big naval guns were being landed from the British Dreadnoughts as they had a superior range to the guns already in use. She was also aware of casualties caused by men who had to stand the shellfire without being able to get in range. She admitted that the German artillery was 'dammed good & marvellously accurate'. On that day she was not on duty but cheerfully wrote that 'there's going to be heaps to do though, and it's topping being up near things & so jolly interesting. About 300 French marched thro' the town today.'

These French forces were to be an important part of Dorothie's war. She recognized the men by their sailors' hats.

Soon she learned that they were called Fusiliers Marins, French sailors with rifles, and quickly shortened their name to Marins. In fact, the Marins were mostly recruited from Brittany and a part of their uniform, the striped Breton fisherman's sweater, is still a fixed uniform piece of the French Navy. Eighty per cent of the men spoke in their Celtic dialect, which contributed to the esprit de corps. The Fusiliers Marins were heading for the forts of Antwerp, but – overtaken by military reality – stopped at Ghent.

To get there, the two Breton regiments had left the railway station of Coudekerque near Dunkirk from midnight on 7 October at intervals in seven trains, the officers in a passenger car, the soldiers in open wagons. Wherever the trains had to stop at stations along the way, the men were greeted by the local Flemish population, sometimes even with the mayor in the lead, and they were offered bread, milk, fruit, and beer. So much beer that one of the last convoys attracted even more public interest by unfurling a French tricolour above a wagon and its flapping accompanied the merry troop. One company accidentally alighted at the station of Furnes and marched towards Ypres, then back to Furnes for a later train. The Fusiliers Marins gradually arrived in Ghent from 4.30 pm on 8 October and they were billeted in the Leopold Barracks, in a nearby girls' school and in the casino, but they were too excited to sleep much. Their commander and his staff moved into the Post Hotel in the centre of town.

The Marins numbered about 6,600 men who were all under the command of a Breton, the 49-year-old Contre-Amiral Pierre-Alexis Ronarc'h. He was a stubborn and proud officer, the right man to lead these men who would literally go through hell for him. A year later, upon his promotion to vice admiral, Dorothie summed him up: 'He was such a nice mixture of capability (from military point of view), courage & absolute simplicity minus all swank, that made all his officers & men worship him, as a result he got everything from his men, where many might have got nothing.'

The two regiments under his command had been hastily improvised, the vast majority being reservists. They also included mechanics, cooks and men from the military administration equipped with rifles. The brigade was first sent directly from the Navy Riflemen School to Paris as a boost for the city's morale against the possibility of another humiliating German occupation. What the Parisians did not know was that half of the rifles of the hastily summoned Fusiliers Marins did not even function properly. However, the long bayonets

Admiral Pierre-Alexis Ronarc'h (1865-1940), Commander of the French Brigade de Fusiliers Marins at the Battle of the Yser in 1914. From 1915 to 1919 he was in command of the naval forces between Nieuwpoort and Antifer, north of Le Havre.

were reassuring. A far-sighted man, Ronarc'h immediately started collecting basic combat equipment for his troops, such as sturdy shoes with studded soles, long coats, proper rifles and ammunition. Long marches and military exercises in the parks of Paris were meant to build an esprit de corps amongst the men. Ronarc'h managed to engender a sense of pride, so that what began as a makeshift army unit grew into an elite corps.

These young men marching through Ghent were very young, some were boys of barely sixteen; even the older ones were only in their twenties. The American war correspondent Arthur Gleason was charmed by the Bretons. He wrote about them in one of his books of war reports, *Golden Lads,* where he called them 'the Play-Boys of the Western Front' because of their youth. He also referred to their nickname: *Les demoiselles au pompon rouge.* (The pompon rouge is the big red dot, officially la houpette, on their seaman's hat, le bachi, officially le bonnet.) It was the fashion-conscious French who came up with that nickname for all those swarthy fellows in their colourful uniforms. According to Gleason,

... they thrust out the face of a youngster from under a rakish blue sailor hat, crowned with a fluffy red button, like a blue flower with a red bloom at its heart. I rarely saw an aging marin. There are no seasoned troops so boyish. They wear open dickies, which expose the neck, full, hard, well-rounded. The older troops, who go laggard to the spading, have beards that extend down the collar; but a boy has a smooth, clean neck, and these sailors have the throat of youth. We must once have had such a race in our cow-boys and Texas rangers — level-eyed, careless men who know no masters, only equals.

The force of gravity is heavy on an old man. But marins are not weighted down by equipment nor muffled with clothing. They go bobbing like corks, as though they would always stay on the crest of things. And riding on top of their lightness is that absurd bright-red button in their cap. The armies for five hundred miles are sober, grown-up people, but here are the play-boys of the western front. (Arthur Gleason *Golden Lads*, 1916, pp.82-3)

Having arrived in Ghent on 8 October, the next day they marched up to the front, attracting massive public interest. The women waved their handkerchiefs and the people cheered 'Vive la France'. 'Vive la Belgique' the French reply. Their destination was the line between the villages of Destelbergen-Melle, Kwatrecht and Gontrode. Marching with them on their right was the Belgian rearguard from the Ghent garrison with about 6000 men. But the fall of the fortresses of Antwerp on their left flank was imminent and the Anglo-Belgian retreat was already in full swing. The German besiegers were preparing to celebrate their victory in the city and Uhlans were raiding the Antwerp countryside. Facing Ronarc'h and his officers the French General Pau left no doubt that the Bretons were to be sacrificed to give the Belgian retreat from Antwerp a chance: 'Look, these are the men who are about to die.'

That very afternoon and night they had to repel four waves of attacking German infantry brought up from Aalst and Moerbeke. Four of the six battalions of Bretons, about 4,000 men, faced 42,000 German infantrymen, who fortunately had no idea of the limited numerical strength of the French and who, like their opponents, had no combat experience. Ronarc'h was careful with the lives of his men and kept one regiment in reserve. He deployed his Marins along a fifteen-mile frontline covering three villages, Gontrode, Kwatrecht and Melle, for the greater part behind a railway embankment. One company was entrenched in shallow pits in the open behind the rails of a railway line. They were immediately blown away by German machine guns – their red pompoms turning them into target practice. However, the bulk of the regiment was safely hidden behind the embankment of the railway from Melle to Mons and quietly pointed their rifles. The German attackers gathered in great numbers in a wood on the other side. Between the opponents lay a beetroot field and meadows. After the first onslaught these were filled with dead and wounded Germans. Exhausted, and with only meagre military rations for food, the Bretons managed to slow down the German advance for twenty-eight hours and gave the bulk of the Belgian army the opportunity to retreat undisturbed towards the Yser river. German losses in casualties and prisoners of war were estimated at 300, a great achievement for two regiments of inexperienced Breton seamen. This first courageous engagement by the Second Regiment of Fusiliers Marins left twelve of them dead, three missing and one a prisoner who managed to escape through the Netherlands and England and back to France. Nine Fusiliers Marins were buried in a row in the municipal cemetery of Melle.

The Fusiliers Marins had their own stretcher-bearers but no motorized ambulances. A local tramway and the ambulances of Munro's Corps brought forty-nine wounded to Ghent (other sources mention forty-eight). The Marins were impressed by the selfless assistance of Munro's men and women and the village of Melle, for its part, did not forget the courage of the Bretons. Dorothie paid her own compliment to the courage of the Marins: 'They are a fine lot these French sailors – pots better than the Belgians.'

After the battle Munro's ambulance corps also collected wounded Germans from among the corpses in the field before the French lines. Dorothie was taking more risks than she admitted in her letters. An officer of the Fusiliers Marins, enseigne de vaisseau Charles Poisson, had spotted her:

The captain sends me off to reconnoitre a farm, from which suddenly two grey uniformed Boches pop up and run away like hares. My men promptly shoot them down, first one, then the other. Behind a pile of straw bales we discover several wounded Germans anxiously staring at us. We want to give them something to drink but they only accept water from their own drinking bottles, perhaps out of fear that we are trying to poison them. I report the place and shortly afterwards an English ambulance takes the risk to come nearer and collect the wounded Germans, thanks to the determination of a nurse whose khaki uniform just made me smile. German corpses are scattered all over the field, quite a lot of them on closer inspection. Two of their reserve officers are lying dead, one on top of the other, at the roadside. A stench hits me as I frisk them for notebooks and military documents. My first close encounter with a dead enemy.

Charles POISSON, Diary of a Marine,

October 1914

47

Dorothie mentioned other dangers:

> These Germans too, you never know they might fire on you
> as you pick 'em up with the result the men do most of that
> work, & I for one don't hold with being potted by a German.
> I don't mind running risks for our men or the French but I'm
> blithered if I'm going to have a hole put in me by a bally Teuton
> whilst I pick up their men. I frankly am not taking any.
>
> Dr. Renton today was fired on by the Germans while getting
> in some of their men. Yesterday near us they put civilians in
> front of the troops again & they were shot by the Belgians
> firing. 2 days ago the Germans near here got 15 of Belgians
> wounded & knocked their heads in.
>
> Lots of cases brought in have evidence conclusive of explosive
> bullets, worse than dum dum being used. They are devils.
>
> [10 October 1914]

The use of explosive bullets that explode inside the body, and
dumdum bullets which fold open on impact, both of which
make terrible wounds, had been considered a war crime since
1868.

On 9 October Antwerp fell and Munro's Corps needed to
retreat. In her letter Dorothie reported the state of confusion
as they had to 'clear out of Ghent in the middle of the night &
since then everything has been chaos & I have had to run the
whole damn show – I wish there was a man with a head in
charge – As soon as I get back I shall settle down & marry a
big strong man who will bully me – I'm sick to death of trying
to run other people.' In a later report Dorothie gave a more
considered reaction:

... it became evident that all the English & French troops the far side of Ghent would have to retreat to prevent them being cut up on the flank. It was a bit 'ard, because at Melle the Germans had been driven back by the French Marines & English troops ... & were very bucked & not at all wanting to retreat. Also it was awful for the poor Belgians, mad with joy when the English arrived to see them retreat after 2 days, & leaving poor little Ghent without so much as firing a shot ... on Monday morning we were told the Teutons were at the gates & all the wounded had to be evacuated. This was done by train to Ostend, except just the English Tommies we were told to take in our ambulances as they were to be kept separate. What a night it was – having to dress them all & pack them & our belongings up. Some of the latter we had to leave behind & trust to getting them after the war. We got the wounded to Eekloo by about 5am & left them to sleep a bit, while we lay on the parlour floor of a neighbouring Englishman's villa & slept like pigs for an hour or two, looking like nothing on Earth sprawling on the carpet. Then on to Bruges and Ostend – having to keep on returning for evacuating troops on the way.

[18 October 1914]

Dorothie was miserable at leaving the town and felt the people of Ghent had been let down, but as the ambulances would have been appropriated and no work left for the Corps, they had no choice. However, she was determined to get back into Ghent with the English army or die in the attempt 'from wrath and indignation if nothing else'.

When they arrived at Ostend it appeared that their part in the war was over for the present – there was no alternative plan and no one knew what to do. However, as it would so many times, Dorothie's extraordinary luck saved the day…

… all the party were squabbling – Munro losing his silly head & running around in circles & there seemed nothing to be done but trek home & try & get out of France – a doubtful event – When I suddenly ran into Thérèse de Broqueville in the street by the purest luck and they were most awfully kind to me & helped me get the ambulance to Dunkerque with the ministry whom leaving the next morning – Such a job as none of them were up – half of them lost & Munro insisting on picking up futile lady pals of his all along the beach & affixing them to our ambulances when we have 3 times as many awful females as we can digest or need… Broqueville has been our guardian angel all along the line & I can't imagine what we would so without him – He & I have just settled things up & this is how the situation stands: Dr Beavis field hospital, late of Antwerp is being attached to Furnes, now Belgian headquarters, & is a moveable affair – Our Ambulance column now consists of 6 ambulances, 4 limousines & 2 open cars is under the command of Robert de Broqueville & attached to the cavalry division – We are 2 in each ambulance with a change of clo' and a toothbrush & no fixed abode & fed up with army rations, in fact like soldiers – Our wounded we take to Beavis field hospital & run in conjunction with him, though he is bound to get other wounded from round about besides what we bring him.

We have got funds between us to look after the wounded from the moment they come into our hands, to when we land them in London, having made arrangements with London hospital to take them in –

It's such a joy to be organised at last – I've got them off
now & under military orders & they will just have to be in
order & run.

[18 October 1914]

Part of Dorothie's recurring good fortune owed a great deal
to her upbringing, education and family friends. She had
been at school in Paris with Thérèse (who married Robert
de Broqueville, the eldest son of the General) and had
stayed with the family many times before the war. Meeting
Thérèse was chance, but it gave Dorothie an opportunity not
to be missed. 'Papa' Broqueville was the Prime Minister of
France and Robert agreed to act as the liaison officer for the
corps. Munro's ambulances were added to the British Field
Hospital for Belgium that had functioned in school buildings
on the Napoleon Quay in Antwerp with a dressing station
in Mechelen. It was then deployed to Furnes and, because it
was considered the best equipped field hospital for the Belgian
army, it was renamed the Belgian Field Hospital. It employed
fifty-four men and women, of whom twelve were doctors and
twenty-five were nurses. Amongst the nurses were Irish, Scots,
and English women and there was also one Dutch nurse, Rosa
Vecht, who had volunteered to serve despite official Dutch
neutrality.

More motor ambulances arrived so that by the end of
October Munro had about a dozen vehicles, half of them
motor ambulances, the rest light trucks and limousines. They
were all gifts and, in some cases, came with the generous donor
as the driver. The Belgian and the French army supplied free
petrol for the ambulance fleet. Dorothie wrote that she was

Charles de Broqueville, Belgian Minister of War. The leader of Belgium's Catholic Party, he was prime minister 1911-1918.

General Hély d' Oissel, Commander of the French Army in the North.

Above: Dorothie in conversation with Belgian soldiers.

Below: Philip Gibbs, British War Correspondent. Dorothie met him 'in the street in tears at not being able to get a journalist's pass, so am going to get him one through Broqueville & he is very pleased.'

so glad that 'our show is on a sound & recognised footing as regards organisation and funds – The latter point has been settled by the Red X London who gave us a quid a week to keep ourselves, so far I had practically no expenses to pay.'

On 25 October in Calais, where Dorothie picked up the additional vehicles, she met Philip Gibbs, the British war correspondent of the *London Daily Chronicle*, again. He was 'in the street in tears at not being able to get a journalist's pass so am going to get him one through Broqueville & he is very pleased. I am running a sort of Bureau at present. Anyone in difficulties comes & bothers me.'

Dorothie was to regret encouraging the press. Gibbs mentioned her in his war reporting, much to her dismay because Dorothie did not want to appear in the press under any circumstances. She considered her war work as her simple duty, and she got enough satisfaction from the sense of having done something significant without having to see it in the newspapers. Thus, she reflected the values of her father, the earl, who also had a profound dislike of frenzied journalistic attention.

Dorothie was furious with Munro and Beavis for encouraging 'tame correspondents' to go about with them:

I am simply crying with rage ... Ashmead Bartlett & Philip Gibbs are glued onto us & I have just been making the hell of a row as having got the old Chronicle with Gibbs' account of Dixmude & dragging me into it all. I think Gibbs was more of a gentleman than to make a fool of me like that, & it makes the whole thing so sordid to look as if we had pet reporter to advertise us ... It is such a shame using me as a lever in this disgusting way ... Oh Mother I am sick over this reporter business – I do hate it – it's so cheap and undoes all the nice feeling one has inside of being able to do something

[27 October 1914]

Unfortunately, Dorothie's war was far from over, and the press were not ready to relinquish a heroine.

3

IN THE THICK OF IT

By 18 October Dorothie and the corps were quartered at the Belgian Field Hospital in Furnes. Even this had been made possible by Dorothie, as this report for 1914 by the headmaster of the local school records:

All of a sudden, in the night 11,400 soldiers burst in, back from Antwerp; classrooms and the reading room were occupied, desks and books were thrown on heaps inside as well as outside and all hope for normal school work had to be given up; the school had been transformed into a barracks overnight.

The fall of Antwerp was a fact; the Belgian army in retreat was on its way to Dunkirk and for the first time the river Yser was being mentioned as a frontline.

A heroic battle was to start along the Nieupoort/Ypres line, Veurne was being dragged into the war for a very long time, the

Catholic school 'The Institute of the Immaculate Conception' was to be fully involved in these times of war ...

Naval guns thundered from the sea and the Pervyse front on that Sunday 18 October when Lady Dorothie arrived and commandeered the school buildings for a field hospital on the authority of an English institution; two days later the upstairs, the downstairs and the outside were teeming with nurses dressed in white and stern-looking English surgeons, the school had metamorphosed. The refectory and the reading room were filled with long rows of maimed soldiers from the Yser front, Belgians, French, Germans next to each other: surgeons worked day and night in the classroom of the sixth-form students, Protestant psalms resonated in another classroom; the courtyard of the primary school was occupied by buzzing automobiles and cheerful drivers.

The students' dormitory was assigned to the nurses and Munro's team found lodgings in the home of a local GP, Dr Joos, close to the bridge on the main road Dunkirk. The doctor and his household had left the house previously and had no idea that it was being occupied by the corps. The house remains there and is still called d'Eedle Rose as it was then, but the British visitors had conveniently renamed it as 'Villa Joos', pronounced as Villa Juice. Munro's team was so numerous that there was little comfort left in the house. Dorothie later recorded those difficult days in her diary:

We were some 16 to 18 people & there were 3 beds! – The way into the house (the keys were lost) was through a back door & then through a broken window – You never saw such a piggery – Beds, stretchers, mattresses & sleeping bags on the floor of the rooms & passages in all directions – I was lucky to have a wee room 10ft by 5 ft about with a mattress on the floor & just room to lie down – The first night we had no blankets to speak of & Helen Gleason & I slept in our clothes & hugged each other like babies for warmth & slept like that! We used to feed at the hospital mess & just stagger up the dark muddy lane to our house & roll into bed – No fire anywhere in the house of course & only ice cold water & no drains! … We get in through the window – the only drawback is that while we are out in the ambulances the French soldiers come in through the window & spend the day in our little beds! OO – ER! – we found it out by their leaving a revolver & a grease mark on the sheets.

However, they were not able to settle in. An angry maid, followed shortly after by Dr Joos and his family, the owners, appeared on the threshold, back from their refuge in France.

Back in Dunkerque for one night on 22 October she wrote a quick report home in which she mentioned the town of Nieuwpoort for the first time and gave her mother a clear picture of what was happening:

Mother dear – It's 1 am & I am very sleepy having slept in my clothes all last night & not washed more than half my neck for a day or two. Just had a bath. Thank God for our good soap. We are quartered at Furnes for the moment as very heavy work round there … All English troops in Belgium now – none in France but Gen French won't advance his army which he meant to do 2 days ago which leaves the hard work for the poor little Belgian army now about 80,000 strong …

French army rotten. Artillery not come up & when it does has no ammunition. Lots of French marines though who are fighting on land & perfect rippers.

[22 October 1914]

Only twelve miles down the front line the 'perfect rippers' were being crushed in the First Battle of the Yser. The Marins had marched without much respite from Melle to Dixmuide and had dug in in a wide circle around the town, manning the areas closest to the river. The flat countryside offered no natural protection for the defenders, and the only obstacles for the attackers were in the form of dense hedges and ditches filled to the brim with water. At their backs the Marins had the meagre safety of the river. The pastures in their line of fire were filled

In the Belgian trenches at Yser. The Battle of the Yser in October 1914 saw the Belgian forces halt the German advance, but at a heavy cost.

General Winter attacks both sides in November 1914. German POWs escorted by British troops.

Würtemberg infantry attempting to cross the Yser on planks are caught in the water let in from the dykes, as illustrated in H. W. Wilson's *The Great War*.

with cattle and sheep and looked peaceful, but refugees reported the arrival of the vanguard of a large German army. The Bretons wisely moved back the next day towards the outskirts of the

Belgian mitrailleur, machine gunner, and fusilier on the Yser, somewhere between Nieuwpoort and Dixmuide.

town of Dixmuide and dug in again, now shoulder-to-shoulder with Senegalese and Belgian battalions. Behind them they anchored a barge across the river as an escape route towards a second battle line on the other side to fall back on. But the French General Foch left no room for manoeuvre: 'The tactic that you must deploy is to resist there where you are.' Suddenly the German sledgehammer smashed the defenders with artillery, heavy machine guns and countless waves of infantry. The Bretons were decimated; on Monday 19 October, 300 were killed. The Germans first broke through the Belgian defence in the middle of the half circle and the 2000 Senegalese Tirailleurs posted alongside, who tried to fill the gap and hold the line at all costs, as ordered, were annihilated. Only 411 of them escaped from this living hell, many wounded but alive.

A brand-new double line of fortresses around Antwerp had barely been able to slow down the German invasion, let alone stop it. How then could an unprotected Dixmuide do so? Leaving the tactical advantage of a town full of tall buildings intact to the enemy had not been an option. Those houses and towers would have given a direct view into the Belgian trenches on the other side of the river and an expansive view of the plains and beyond. However, during the battle for Dixmuide the German artillery demolished the greater part of the buildings anyway.

Munro's ambulances were in the thick of it and came to fetch the wounded Belgians, Marins and Senegalese, day and night; first from the town hall, to which the wounded had been brought from every corner of the town and later, when collapsing houses and a rain of shells made the town inaccessible, the ambulances waited for the wounded at the bridge across the river. The last two miles to the bridge were constantly under German artillery fire and for safety reasons the ambulances had to approach without lights, but the burning village of Kaaskerke and farms on fire on both sides of the road shed light for them to and from Dixmuide. Glass shards caused frequent punctures and sparks made the journey even more risky.

The members of the Munro Corps managed to stay more or less unharmed during that terrible month of the battle of the Yser, but two of their drivers were injured: John Secker was hit by a shell splinter but doggedly continued to drive to Furnes with his cargo of wounded, and Eustace Gurney received a stray bullet in his leg but carried on despite his wound. Much later, in November 1916, Gurney would escape once again when a shell exploded next to his ambulance at a dressing station in Nieuwpoort hurling chunks of earth and shrapnel across the driver's seat but failing to hit him.

Most of the time, Dorothie drove her ambulance assisted by Robert de Broqueville. As mentioned, Robert's father was the Belgian Prime Minister, and the family were close friends of the Feildings. On other occasions Dorothie drove a touring car, a Rolls-Royce which she referred to as a limousine. It was certainly faster and more agile than the big, clumsy motor-ambulances. The idea was to get as close as possible to the firing line, hastily load the wounded – those who could sit up were put in the front seat, stretcher-cases put across the back of the car – and drive as quickly back to the motor ambulances waiting further down the road, out of sight but not out of reach of the German artillery. The car should have been driven by the Belgian chauffeur as women were still not allowed near the front, but he 'has cold feet & funks – so when it gets exciting he gets down at the roadside – I drive on & collect the 'blessés' & then pick up my chauffeur on the way home – It's killing & makes everyone die with laughter.' Then the wounded were carefully transferred to the ambulances, which set off for the field hospital in Furnes, about ten miles from Nieuwpoort. The transport across the bumpy and slippery roads was a continuation of their suffering and the cobblestone roads full of shell holes, debris and scrap metal made it a hellish ride.

… no lights of course near the lines & only room on the pavé
for one vehicle at a time – At each side deep, slimy mud, in pot
holes – To get your wheel off the edge of the pavé meant untold

suffering & jolting to the men on the stretchers within & yet this had to be done each time anything was passed & in the dark it was a nightmare.

[30 October 1914]

Despite these difficulties, Dorothie was always aware of the comfort of her wounded passengers and took great care to avoid jolting the vehicle if at all possible. Unsurprisingly, women ambulance drivers were preferred because they drove more cautiously.

Dixmuide was attacked on 16 October and was defended by Belgian and French troops under Colonel Alphonse Jacques, who would later be awarded the title 'de Dixmude' for his role in the defence of the town. On 18 October, the German offensive began and overran Allied troops from Nieuwpoort south to Arras in France. The objective was to defeat the Belgian and French armies and to deprive the British of access to Calais, Boulogne and Dunkirk. The Third Reserve Corps attacked Belgian defences from Dixmuide to the sea, regardless of loss. The Germans captured advanced posts at Keiem, Schoore and part of Mannekensvere and reached the Yser, despite fire support from the Anglo-French flotilla, which bombarded German troops along the coast.

On 21 October, the Germans were able to establish a small bridgehead on the west bank of the Yser, despite a counterattack by the French 42nd Division, and the last bridge was blown up on 23 October. Dixmuide bore the brunt of repeated German offensives and bombardments, yet the town was still not taken. The French high command planned to flood large parts of their territory as a defensive measure.

This would have given the Belgian army the impossible choice of being trapped between the flood and the Germans, or else abandoning the last part of unoccupied Belgium. The plan was postponed, since the Belgian army had started preparations to flood the area between the Yser and its tributary canals. On 25 October, the German pressure on the Belgians was so great that a decision was taken to flood or inundate the entire Belgian front line. After an earlier failed experiment on 21 October, the Belgians managed to open the sluices at Nieuwpoort during the nights of 26–29 October during high tides, steadily raising the water level until an impassable flooded area was created about one mile wide, stretching as far south as Dixmuide.

Despite this, the Germans launched another large attack on the Yser on 30 October. It punched through the Belgian second line and reached Ramskapelle and Pervijze but was stalled by Belgian and French counterattacks, which recovered Ramskapelle. The final attack, planned for the next day, was called off when the attacking Germans became aware of the flooding of the land in their rear. They withdrew the night before 31 October.

Dorothie noted the successes of the Belgian defence: 'Belgians done very well – 500 Germans crossed the river this morning [22 October] but were all shot & prisonered & Belgians now in strong positions on far side of river.' Some of the German prisoners of war were stowed in the front of the ambulances and deposited in the courtyard of the hospital. It was the first time that the corps members had encountered such large numbers of Germans POWs and their presence caused a great deal of excitement. Elsie Knocker, Dorothie's colleague, even cut a button off a German sleeve as a souvenir. Everyone wanted to have their picture taken with a prisoner, probably to send home as some kind of proof of the danger of their work, but not Dorothie. She was, as always, more interested in finding out the truth: 'One man I talked to left Berlin 5 days ago and was taken prisoner today without firing a shot. Another came from Ghent & one of the blighters who chased us away. Please God we shall soon be back.' (22 October 1915.)

In another letter a few days later she added some more details.

Day before yesterday 5 of our ambulances only brought in 157 people from one side of the front & those other direction ditto. It's awful – the desperate cases we have at the hospital here and all possible we send on by train 2 days ago 4,500 wounded passed through Furnes. This war is a nightmare just – I can't see when it is to end.

The patients were being sent on by train to the next Belgian military hospital, which was in Calais. Each day a locomotive with a long row of cattle trucks waited on a sidetrack for its load of suffering. There was no light, no water, no stretchers, no blankets, just straw and the soaked, muddy, bloodied greatcoats as protection against the cold. It took the trains three to four days to get there because there was only a single railway track across the border between Belgium and France and any army trains directed to the front had priority. Moreover, French officials tended to give priority to French trains over Belgian ones. Trains loaded with wounded had to wait idly for hours in the stations of Veurne and Adinkerke where they were easy targets for German aircraft. Hundreds of French wounded were unloaded in two locomotive sheds at the railway station of Dunkirk that had to pass for a casualty clearing station but, except for straw on the floor, lacked almost everything, including hot water. The English war artist and volunteer ambulance driver Christopher R.W. Nevinson, painted the gloomy interior of one of those sheds in his painting *La Patrie*, now in the Birmingham City Art Gallery and Museum.

Paul Sauvaire Jordan of the 1st Regiment Cuirassiers, assigned to the Fusiliers Marins as a machine gunner, described how Munro's ambulances came to pick him up for a long and painful journey across the cobblestone road in a letter home: 'These damned Belgian roads are quite unsuited for the wounded. I have passed an awful hour on them, even with a driver who drove very slowly.' Presumably, this was one of those female drivers.

Although the journey was only seven miles it could take as long as an hour. As he was not seriously injured, he was dropped off at the station of Veurne. He was given a cup of cold coffee in the station and some hot broth later during the journey. He was unloaded in Dunkirk and dumped in the hall of the station, then, at 10 pm the next day, back on a train to the French hospital ship *Ceylan* in the port of Calais. On the hospital ship, his wounds were dressed again. There were more than a thousand injured on board and in addition to the pain and the crowding, high waves made the 48-hour trip appalling as just about everyone was seasick. The ship docked in Saint-Nazaire on 18 December at midnight, as moving the wounded overnight hid the disturbing sight from the civilian population. In Saint-Nazaire, the wounded were loaded into cattle cars, which had no shock absorbers and rattled along the rails, torturing the passengers on their stretchers. 'My leg jumped up and down, each time hitting the wooden bar of the stretcher... You cannot imagine how much pain I have suffered there.' This new suffering was so unbearable for all the wounded on board that after half an hour somebody ordered the train to halt and the wounded were brought to the nearest military hospital, No. 14, in Savenay instead of the one in Pontivy, another 6½ hours away. It was in Savenay that Paul wrote his report to his father. He added that he would keep his sou'wester with a bullet hole as a souvenir and hoped to recover quickly so as to be able to settle his account with *les Boches*.

Back in October 1914, during the Battle of the Yser, Arno Dosch-Fleurot, an American war correspondent, saw Dorothie on her way to the village of Ramskapelle, then heavily shelled, an ordeal which he had been observing from a cottage near the canal.

> On our way back to the safety of the dunes a motorized Red Cross ambulance came towards us. Next to the driver sat a young English woman. She wore a gray-brown overcoat and gray-brown leggings as British soldiers do. We shouted to her that we thought the village was deserted, but the only response from the ambulance flying past was the raised hand of the young woman who thus expressed that she knew all too well what she was doing.

Indeed, on the night of 29 to 30 October, that same young woman was with Dr Munro at the edge of a burning

Ramskapelle, in a country pub that served as a dressing station. In the village centre just down the road a fierce hand-to-hand fight between the Germans and Belgian, French, and Algerian troops was raging. The ominous sounds of bullets hitting stone and the rattle of machine-guns were clearly audible. Inside the pub, a steady stream of wounded arrived in need of urgent help. Dorothie expressed her impatience with the conditions and was not afraid of criticising those she felt were not up to her standard:

> The military doctor was a fool & Munro & I had to dress several very bad fractures by the light of one candle as no big light was allowed & we had to bring ambulances up in the dark as we always do at night for the last 5 miles or so. It was an extraordinary sight in there in the half light, black men & white men & tired out soldiers all lying about on the straw poor devils.

The number of soldiers brought was more than the hospital could cope with:

> The numbers made it possible for the hospital at Furnes only to take in the practically dying men – All the rest had to go by train & what trains – Not well arrayed Red X trains ... but goods trains & even cattle trucks with a little dirty straw & no light or water or any doctoring to speak of – As soon as a train was full, it would be shunted out, but perhaps only to remain on the sidings for many hours – It took as a rule 3 to 4 days before the men got to hospital at Calais some 40 miles back.

Only three thousand from over six thousand men in the Brigade survived the first hour of the Battle for Dixmuide. Of the other half, some were killed or wounded, some taken prisoner and others simply went missing, probably crushed and buried under burning and collapsing buildings. Despite these events, at the end of that murderous week Dorothie still estimated the morale of the battered survivors at eighty per cent. But fighting spirit was not enough to make a significant impact on events. Although the German army never succeeded in crossing the Yser, it remained on the far side of the river for the rest of the war. Stalemate had set in.

The front behind Dixmuide became relatively stable during November and the remnants of the Marins were pulled back, to be replaced by other troops. Dorothie reported the arrival of Senegalese troops at Dixmuide. The French were calling troops from all their colonies to help in the war and these troops had arrived in late October: 'As black as ink & on mules with the weirdest eastern effect – They give one no end of a turn in the dark as they creep by.'

Once the emergency of the battle had subsided Dorothie's attention could return to more mundane and less critical matters. She found time to complain about one of her colleagues, a driver, Mr Johnyson from Dunchurch, who '... has been seedy & obliged to go home. Also he loses his head in an emergency ... the moment there was a black maria in sight he got in a sort of faint & utterly collapsed.' She asked her mother if she could spare Smee, the Feilding chauffeur, and suggested that she should warn him that he might get shot at – 'If he thinks he would mind going into a tight corner now & then it's no earthly use his coming – but I think his heart's alright & he's such a hard working little devil he'd be a treasure.'

Even very ordinary commodities were luxuries in a war zone. At home, daily bathing was routine but here hot water was in short supply and when it could be obtained was worthy of comment. Dorothie liked to be clean and often reported when she managed to obtain some hot water. Prince Alexander of Teck, a member of the British royal family, was a long-standing friend and Dorothie was delighted to find him serving in Belgium, for not only did he provide charming and entertaining company, often inviting her to dine, but he also offered her the use of his bath.

Dorothie also had time to take hundreds of photographs with her small Kodak camera and she sent the negatives home to be developed. She attached descriptions so that her family would understand what they were looking at. For example, she wrote of the Marins:

> Whenever they see us they dash for us & give us coffee & food & letters to post for them & whenever they are in trouble with wounded & no one will take an ambulance up to them, they always come to us & we give them a hand –They fight like little lions & are such nice simple souls & so grateful & nice manners – In that they resemble the Belgian Tommies – The French Tommies (not the Marins) are an odious bunch – rude & unobliging.

Dorothie's admiration for the Marins – often to the detriment of other soldiers – shines through her letters.

There was one soldier, though, for whom Dorothie had an even greater affection. She was very happy to hear that her brother Rollo's regiment had transferred from Aisne in Picardy, and was now in Belgium, based at Ypres and therefore in visiting distance. She made frequent attempts to meet him, but on 2 November she was unsuccessful because the English authorities would not let her pass because she was female. She threatened to hide in the car and put on a khaki coat to get close enough to get news. Instead, she went to get information from the headquarters of the 2nd Division, who were quartered at a chateau on the Hooge–Ypres road. She arrived just after a terrible explosion that had killed six members of the headquarters staff and wounded ten more. The tragedy was that amongst the dead was one of her best friends, Captain Rupert Ommanney. The official history describes the circumstances:

About 1.15pm shortly after a low flying enemy aeroplane has passed over, a shell fell into the chateau grounds some 20-30 yards in front of the coach house. A minute later another burst immediately outside General Monroe's room followed by a third which struck the glass roof of the studio, and a fourth which dropped in the grounds. The second shell fell on the assembled staffs. Major Gen Lomax was severely wounded and died some months later in England. There were killed on the spot Col F W Kerr and Major G Paley of the General Staff of 1st Div.

This unfortunate incident could not have happened at a worse moment. The meeting of the senior staff officers happened at the height of the German assaults along the Menin Road at Gheluvelt, and arguably the loss of the senior staff officers disrupted the command structure.

British casualties later at the Menin Road.

Captain Rupert Ommanney's death caused great distress to Dorothie. She confided in her mother that it was awful and that it haunted her because she had arrived at the chateau one hour after he was killed and was not aware of it until the next day. What made it worse was that she received a letter from him the very night she had found out about his death. She asked her mother to pray for him: 'I know you never quite approved of him but I did & he was one of my best friends – I have felt so much not being able to see him this year past.'

All the deaths and the constant wretchedness of war around her were beginning to affect her resilience.

It's awful this war – everyday one hears of all one's pals of the day before that have gone – At times when one was standing alongside them perhaps only for a few hours or minutes before – it seems hard to believe the appalling rapidity with which one can be moved off the face of the earth.

Dorothie often became exasperated by the rules and regulations which seemed to her to be petty, pointless and inefficient. In early November she made another attempt to see Rollo by making an assignation with a Royal Army Medical Corps (RAMC) man who agreed to take her and Robert to the Coldstream Guards trenches. She was desperate for a 'chinwag' with Rollo but was foiled again, by Captain Fitzpatrick, who

... dashed up, was frightfully rude to us & Broqueville & tried to arrest us for working in the English lines without being 'army'. He turned us out of Ypres before I could meet my doctor & go up to Tubby – It was disgusting too because we were doing work that no one else was – Gleason got some people off up by Rollo's people that had been there 2 days & all the men & officers just implored us to come back – I & Robert got a lot of Irish Guards in from a cottage near their trenches, in the dark, dodging caverns in the roads made by shells that evening – We got two loads away & had promised to come back for the others when Fitzpatrick refused to let us go on working & we had to go knowing the poor devils would probably be left there for hours until they were brought off on an old horsecart that jolted like mad & lucky if they were fetched at all.

Dorothie just refused to give up! On 7 November she tried again to see Rollo on a quiet day but this time:

....came in for the big shells at Ypres between 5 and 6 p & jolly near got snookered too – The Almighty looks after us very nicely, I had left the car alongside a building, then saw the English officer coming who had been so rude to us the day before, so hurriedly took the car & hid round the corner – Just after the first big shell came phut exactly where our car had been & so I am rather grateful to that officer for having made a nuisance of himself the day before – We picked up some men that were wounded by that shell & were running them round to a hospital when another came & dropped between our car & Dr Munro who was following us on the pavement – It knocked him down but luckily didn't hurt him – Then we had some more exciting moments as, having mislaid Dr Munro, we couldn't leave our post until he turned up & our pew happened to be the cathedral at which they were aiming!

Although Dorothie frequently reassured her mother that she was safe and taking care, this sort of information would surely have caused concern. Dorothie's tone was light and entertaining, but she was taking risks and putting a lot of trust in the Almighty to take care of her. Her faith was very deep and although she had many very close brushes with death she was not seriously injured during the whole time in Flanders.

Perhaps her mother wrote of her concerns as in the next few letters Dorothie told her parents that things were much quieter – in fact stalemate – and that the Germans had taken all their artillery and spare men down to Ypres where the big struggle was then taking place. She was still haunted by Ommanney's death, obviously unable to get it of her mind, and, knowing the battles were going to continue and more men were going to die, in a black moment expressed despair: 'I wish to God it were over.'

Dorothie was not the only one to feel the stress. Doctors and nurses were not prepared for the kind of injuries that were caused by explosive shells or the diseases of trench life, nor with the overwhelming number of victims. The correct medical equipment was not available or not yet invented. War surgery had to be learned by practice. From their experience in the Boer War in the Transvaal, the RAMC was initially convinced that 30,000 beds would suffice for the duration of this new war on the Continent. Eventually 600,000 beds would be barely enough. Doctors who had been at work in a civilian hospital or in a GP's office a month before were suddenly faced with medical military orders that were contrary to their Hippocratic Oath. Only the wounded with a reasonable chance of recovery, and thus front-line service, were to be treated immediately. The heavily wounded were given painkillers and left to die in a corner. Soldiers with severe abdominal wounds were given up at once as there was too little chance of recovery. It took a sixteen-year-old French soldier with an abdominal wound days to die in the hospital at Veurne. It would be 1916 before French and Belgian army doctors would be allowed to treat abdominal wounds, while the same surgeons did exactly that in their civil practice – often with success.

Conditions in the hospital at Furnes from 18 October to 15 January were described by an English nurse, Dorothy Yates:

It becomes almost monotonous to tell you again that all those hundreds and hundreds of men we nursed were far spent – suffering from shock collapse, excessive haemorrhage, broken to pieces, many mortally wounded, all in agony, suffering from cold, hunger, exposure to winter weather, frost bite, and every evil that can bring strong men to death's door. We had also a new trouble to contend with, gangrene had broken out, often of a malignant description. We isolated these and amputated limbs where possible to save them.

Tetanus appeared, but we soon obtained serums from England and gave all patients with wounds covering large surfaces a preventive injection. Often large pieces of clothing were embedded in wounds, to say nothing of shrapnel and mud. From beneath one man's shoulder-blade we even extracted a large brass time-fuse! We had one wonderful case of recovery in our large ward; an officer, with the rank of Major, was brought in with huge wounds in his abdomen, while his intestines were absolutely riddled with shot. The surgeons cut out twelve feet of entrails, and he made an excellent recovery! This was the more remarkable considering that all the patients surrounding him were suffering from dirty and festering wounds, and at that time we had no means of sterilizing the ward dressings. Later on we had large steam sterilizers in the theatre.

Stretchers arrived constantly, borne by Red-Cross orderlies. We were used to death and dying at our hospital, but here we met despair. Most of those lying on that straw were in extremis – nothing could be done for them, grey ashen faces looked dully at us, they were mostly too bad to groan. It is dreadful to be impotent, to stand by grievously stricken men it is impossible to help, to see the death-sweat gathering on young faces, to have no means of easing their last moments. This is the nearest to Hell I have yet been. We put all the hopeful cases into our cars, driving one or two loads to the little station, and then returning for more, which we took back with us to Furnes.

That night, among our wounded soldiers, lay two little children and a young woman. A tot of two years old had both feet blown off; a little girl of four was minus an arm, and the woman had her leg blown off just below the hip and her arm broken.

Dorothie's care and devotion to her 'blessés' was observed by Cora Maine, an Irish nurse at the Belgian Field Hospital:

Lady Dorothie Feilding ... always came to look for me whenever she brought in a load of wounded. She had a notion that I knew best what was to be done for all the varied cases & she said I kept my head & my humanity better than most folk. I admit I had much to thank her for in many ways, little incidents of sympathy & understanding that seemed to give us trust and encouragement in each other. She was an excellent linguist & was useful to me on many occasions. She would come & take messages to send to French & Belgian relatives, nothing was too much trouble for her. She would stay up all night if she could be of the slightest use & always of course if there was or had been any fighting. It was a great pleasure to me to meet and to work with such people.

The stress, the cold military logic, the continuing madness and their own exhaustion resulted in heavy infighting among some nurses and doctors. As 1914 drew to a close, Dorothie commented on the tension to her mother, 'had to stop at Furnes to make the peace as usual', and later, on 30 December, she described the situation to her father:

> I have left the cave for a bit – I find if I am away for long I lose touch with the crowd here & they squabble & mess things up, whereas for some marvellous reason I seem to be the only person none of them want to kick or bite! So when I come I find I can often persuade them to bury hatchets & work in harmony. I have been here at our headquarters now for 2 days.

The tension was exacerbated by shortages of basic supplies and inefficiencies in the supply chain. Dorothie had written to Dr Evans asking for India rubber air pillows, but as the Red Cross had already sent them, she asked that the £10 should be sent to Alexander of Teck for 200 sheets and some chloroform: 'The sheets are appallingly wanted.' She told Teck she would beg the money off people, including her friends. Bobbie Cassel had sent her some leather lining for her clothes, and Dorothie asked: '... if there is anything else she or anyone else wants to give I would love some cases containing each a hypodermic syringe & some tubes of morphia & spare needles. Anything from one to 15 or more of these I can find happy homes for at the various little dressing stations near the front.'

Still in shock about Ommanney's death she received more bad news – her sister Marjie's future husband, Dudley Hanly, had been wounded. It was only slight, but Dorothie must have been distressed as the war was now closely affecting her family and friends. She also felt deeply for the soldiers suffering from the bad weather: 'This wet is hell for the poor tommies in the trenches. It's awful to see the state they are in from it & it takes the heart out of a man to be frozen & soaked & never able to dry. It's sadder even than the wounded somehow to see the state they are in.'

Dorothie and the Munro corps were able to provide some comfort. By 21 November, the corps had moved and Dorothie wrote that they were 'camped in a cellar at Pervyse', and as they had no wounded they thought they might as well do something. There was snow and ice everywhere and it was so cold there was very little doing as far as fighting was concerned.

'It's not luxury but there is a very fine cellar intact where me, Mrs Knocker, Mrs Gleason, a chauffeur & 2 soldiers all sleep in a row on some straw as snug as bugs – we make huge cauldrons of Irish stew stuff all day – It cooks all night & we take it to the trench men as soon as it's light.'

When Dorothie was not involved in making Irish stew or soothing ruffled feathers at the hospital she was still 'Rollo hunting'. This time she was determined to find him as he was to receive the Distinguished Service Order (DSO) for conspicuous gallantry in leading a platoon during an attack on 2 October near Stroombeck.

On 7 December, Dorothie wrote joyfully to her father that she had been having huge fun with Rollo and his wife, Mellins who was also there to see the presentation.

It does one good to be with one's own belongings again you know & everyone here has been too nice to us – We started off by hiding on all fours under the bed and pretending to be ___! & ended up by going the round all of the messes & being given vast dinners by all the colonels we had started off by being frightened of – The result was instead of staying 2 days we have stayed a week – But we felt justified on account of dear old Tubby getting his DSO – 'George' pinned it on himself the other morning at Hazebrouck & Mellins & I hid in a doorway only a few yards off & watched it all, which was splendid.

Modestly, Rollo could not understand why he had been awarded the medal but Dorothie thought it was obvious after hearing his fellow officers describe how he had been running things 'all that sticky 5 weeks'.

It was a very happy week for Dorothie, who had been feeling depressed and sad about the war situation and the deaths of dear friends. The three of them 'had been as snug as bugs in the digs in the village and had just loafed around & felt happy'. And, although Dorothie was very popular with all levels of society and was caring, loving and generous with her time, she confided in her father: 'It is so restful being with just with one's own 'éspèce' again – You don't realise till you get away from them, how trying it is being months at a time without people of one's own walk of life, however excellent the others may be individually.'

Lady Denbigh had also visited that week and Dorothie wanted to reassure her mother that she really had a good restful week and was feeling happy: 'We have had great fun dodging Generals & Brigadiers & people & be being tactful & being prepared to "evacuate" at a minute's notice – It was so nice having you these days & this week of seeing you all has bucked me up no end.'

Restored, Dorothie was soon back to work. There were continuing skirmishes from which the ambulance corps collected the wounded and took them to dressing stations. In a letter printed in the *Rugby Advertiser* on 12 December, Captain Carter, RAMC, reported:

> While some fierce fighting was going on I, with other stretcher bearers, was out collecting wounded and at a small dressing station we were assisted by a lady whom you will no doubt know, Lady Dorothie Feilding, the daughter of the Earl of Denbigh. She was not at a base, but at a small cottage with her motor-ambulance, with shells flying around, and she did some excellent work in transporting the sick to hospital. She is a lady of whom Britain may well be proud.

The countess would have been proud, but she was also anxious for news. As she had not heard from Dorothie, she sent her daughter an indignant letter accusing her of not writing. Dorothie was quick to reply and explain that it was because of the censors who had been holding up letters. To put her mind at rest even more, she also advised her mother that the story of Pervyse being attacked by rafts was pure myth. But Dorothie was mistress of the understatement. Having attempted to assuage her mother's concerns she spoiled the effect by describing, 'a goodly few old shrapnel flying round lately – but nothing to fret about'. A few days later she told her mother:

> I am very well – only very dirty – You should just see my neck! – These bally Germans have been throwing a lot of

things at us lately – As I write I am warming my toes over the fire, & there is a lot of shrapnel fuzzing around – Bang – There's another – It's another – Bang! – Buts it's extraordinary how little damage they do – The trenches are more or less shrapnel proof & very snug.

The countess may or may not have been reassured by her daughter's sangfroid.

By 22 December, Dorothie and the corps had been at Pervyse a month. They were very fit but 'oh so dirty'. As long as there was no heavy fighting they could really do a lot of work running the dressing station and the regiments were very grateful. Rather worryingly, Dorothie reported that four shells actually landed in the trenches, which was a new occurrence. The shells damaged the corner of the 'the cave' and made a mass of shrapnel holes in the bonnet of the old Daimler. But Dorothie finished the letter on a cheerful note:

Our only tragedy at Perveyse [*sic*] is our water supply – The only water comes from the cemetery yard where 358 Germans are 'interred' –Yesterday the pump stuck & has not worked since & it is feared a Teuton has worked his way up the spout – General disgust but no one is brave enough to look & see – Meanwhile water is getting scarce.

Probably for the first time in her life Dorothie did not spend Christmas with her family at Newnham Paddox. Instead, she was writing to them from a little dressing station whilst she warmed her toes. She and all her companions expected that it would be a peaceful day:

> We thought the Teutons would have the decency to leave us in peace, as we expected they would be just as excited over their plum pudding as we over ours – but blessed if the offensive blighters didn't spend the whole morning throwing shrapnel and shells at us, having gone to the trouble to bring a gun up closer under cover of fog – a really dirty trick & most unchristmassy I consider.

The Munro Corps planned to have a Christmas dinner and was given a bottle of 'pluz' by the officers. They had been giving large quantities of clothes to the various regiments and had received touching letters saying how much the soldiers loved the members of the corps. They had also a variety of food for Christmas which had been sent to Munro and he had given his ladies a most generous share. Dorothie received lots of letters from her family, with photos and a pair of mittens from Taffie, one of the younger sisters. Dorothie, of course, planned to 'find someone with cold hands to give them to'. She also had a 'killing letter from Hughie, furious at his being on the equator while a "young upstart like me" is on the spot!' Then there was a dressing to perform on a soldier 'with the unromantic complaint of boils – a messy performance'. The corps went out collecting shrapnel heads and shells and Dorothie reported that they were very merry and she felt that they were friends and, tongue in cheek, that she was having a much nicer Christmas than her family at home.

On 28 December Dorothie wrote to her mother thanking her for the parcels and the villagers of Monks Kirby for all their gifts, and told her mother that she was touched by their kindness. She finished the last letter of 1914 to her mother with the promise of a prayer: 'Goodbye Mother darling I will pray so hard for you all this Xmas & that your heartache for the boys won't be too great – I wish to God this war was over – poor little Mother.'

4

OLD ALBERT'S BIT OF TIN

As 1914 gave way to 1915, the sense of excitement and adventure felt by Dorothie and millions of others gradually gave way to exhaustion, loss, and a sense of futility. For Dorothie, snatched moments of rest and distraction from the business of war were becoming more and more precious.

Although her mother and Mellins had just returned home from a visit to the front, Dorothie was looking forward to a visit to Newnham Paddox for the wedding of Marjie to Dudley Hanly on 18 January, and she intended to stay a week. She had not been home for five months and was aching to see her brother Hugh again. Marjie and Dudley had only been engaged a short time but wanted to disregard the protocol of a long engagement and get married quickly and Dorothie understood – she had seen so many deaths, several of close friends and people she loved, and had just heard about the death of one of Rollo's friends. 'What it must mean to Rollo

King Albert and Queen Elisabeth vising the trenches on the Yser Front.

Periscope view over the barricades.

is too awful – poor boy – The horror of seeing one's pals drop out like that.' Still distressed by the death of Rupert Ommanney, she saw no point in waiting. 'In this awful war one just has to snatch any minute of happiness one can before it melts & a week or two more or less would mean an enormous difference to them.'

Dorothie went home to her sister's wedding and returned to the Front on 24 January, to hear that Furnes had been shelled all week and the wounded had been moved from the hospital; things sounded very bad. However, she was relieved to find the hospital staff and the ambulance corps still there and that a new site for the hospital had been found – a convent about seven miles up the Ypres Road. The town had suffered little damage, but the population had been cleared out and, as it been decided that it was not safe to keep the wounded in the vicinity, there was no use for the hospital. Nonetheless, thinking ahead, it was possible they could open it up again, so a few nurses and other people stayed there to use it as a 'poste de secours' (dressing station) and also make sure 'no one else bags the building'. The Corps had to move all the equipment to the convent and Dorothie felt 'sick at losing this as a base but hope to return if the Teuton's guns that go for it can be silenced'.

After her rest at home, it was annoying to find there had been these changes, but she was overjoyed to learn that General Roger Hély d'Oissel was going to command that part of the French line, 'which is splendid, & he will also facilitate our ambulance work which is no small consideration as we often "come up" against fussy little French officers.' D'Oissel was the father of Suzanne, Dorothie's best friend at the Paris convent and Dorothie knew him well.

Dorothie frequently commented with some asperity that she wished she could manage the 'whole dam show'. The Corps had just settled into a routine when they were informed of new orders. The Red Cross told them that in March they would have to withdraw all ambulances lent to the French and Belgians as everything they had, and more, was required by Kitchener's new army. The Corps would have to collect funds immediately to replace the three cars that did not belong to them and accept any offers of really good cars that could be converted into ambulances. Already busy with the daily work of collecting the wounded, Dorothie now had to take on the task of raising more money. The Red Cross office in London began to write to the City Companies such as the Fishmongers and Goldsmiths Companies, asking for 'pennies from their charity funds'. Dorothie used all the means available to her, her aristocratic background and the family's contacts. She asked her father if the Joint Stock or Rio Tinto companies would like to give them something. 'I am writing to you because I know you won't do anything if you think it's indiscreet, but on the other hand I feel sure some of your city pals will agree!'

Dorothie had enjoyed her trip home and told her father, 'It was good to see you again & I just loved my week at home – really I congratulate myself more each time on my choice of parents.' To her mother: 'It was so nice to be home again & see all your dear faces. Real amazing luck to fall upon you all there in a lump.' Now she was back in the thick of it she apologised for being remiss in her letter writing, 'owing to change in hospitals & places things have been one dam thing after another', and assured her mother 'It's 3 days now since we had a shell in Furnes & things are very snug again.' A shell had hit the hospital and burst in the courtyard, although only the washing had been wrecked, no one was hurt as the nurses had been evacuated. Having assured her mother all was well, Dorothie then told her that one of their nurses had been killed during the bombardment.

The Belgians had taken on a lot of French trenches on the far side of Dixmuide, from Steenstrade and Binchote. Dorothie was pleased not only that d'Oissel was commander of the division by Nieuwpoort but also that he had all the Fusilier Marins with him, 6,000 of them. They asked Dorothie and the Corps to dine with them. She commented that they

… have been charming … & making everything smooth & easy, & so grateful – Such a difference after all the troubles we have had here with these swine of French infantry doctors who consider

Time for sport: Fusiliers about to career down a cobbled street full of shell holes in a Canadian canoe fitted on to perambulator wheels, complete with a double-bladed paddle.

they do you a favour by allowing you to get obussed [shelled] getting their wounded when they haven't the spunk to go in & do it themselves ... Those sailors are ripping to work for & such gentlemen – I can't stick the French infantry at any price.

[2 February 1915]

A salute for the camera: 'longest way up, shortest way down'.

The arrival of another of her favourite people added to Dorothie's happiness. 'My old "dispatches" pal Admiral Ronarch is back there too under Hély d'Oissel.' He was there as commander of the Marins responsible for the defence of the Lombard to St George line and the French infantry dune. Dorothie described it as 'the very devil that dune & almost impossible to take – It's a natural fortress – after an attack the other day there that cost them 300 men they had to give up the trench they took as it was untenable from mines.' 300 deaths of her beloved Marins added to her grief.

On 3 February her bravery was recognised and Dorothie with typical Denbigh insouciance wrote that: '"Old Albert" gave me a tin cross today which I am putting up for auction – what offers? ... The dear man was very kind & said many nice things – Told me Bridges was trying to send us home & was much amused & said he would leave us as we were.'

'Old Albert' was the King of the Belgians, and the tin cross was the Order of Leopold, awarded for extreme bravery in combat or for meritorious service of immense benefit to the Belgian nation. Dorothie sounded offhand and dismissive, but she was always embarrassed when she was publicly thanked or rewarded. Of course, the family knew the king personally and this may have been a family nickname for him – these letters were not meant to be read by anyone but her mother. Dorothie considered it was her duty to serve her country, but she was not happy, in fact hated any sort of publicity and admiration of her war work that praised her commitment and drew attention to her; the only publicity she sought was for donations of money or equipment for her beloved tommies, the Marins and any other wounded soldiers. A few days later she asked her mother to get someone to send over 'a large size primus stove to burn petrol (paraffin no can get) ... we have nothing in our case of the sort & it's imperative for heating things quick at night & at odd times'. It must have been frustrating that this far into the war there was no official supply chain to send vital medicines such as morphine, equipment such as hypodermic needles, and basic items of clothing. Relying on one's friends and contacts owing to the chaos and lack of organisation in the War Office made things even more arduous for those who were at the Front face to face with death and injury. These soldiers were sacrificing their lives for their country and such a lack of concern showed a callous disregard for their loyalty.

Dorothie would not miss a chance to visit her family and she planned to snatch more leave to attend Mollie's wedding. She was 'longing for a hunt ... I am very weary, very bad tempered, very headachy & oh so longing for a little peace right way from everyone & everything for 48 hrs ... I do so hate this eternal evacuating – it always gives me the blues.' Their accommodation had been shelled, which had forced them to leave, and they were temporarily by the sea, a long way from the hospital. After what seemed to Dorothie an interminable delay, she was overjoyed to hear the wedding had finally been arranged for 25 February. 'I am longing for a few days mental peace more that I have ever since the beginning of the war I think.'

Dorothie was working hard in terrible weather conditions; very wet, everywhere a sea of mud and out most nights until midnight getting the wounded back to hospital. In the daytime there was little time to rest as the Germans were shelling and she was forced to seek shelter at the hospital. Always practical,

Dorothie grabbed her washing, tied it up in a red handkerchief, '& fled up the street like a stag... You would have laughed to see me. There is always that to be said that whenever you are the most frit there is nearly always something especially ludicrous that happened to make one laugh. That's providence I suppose.'

Dorothie managed to get her leave and went home to see Mollie and Cecil married. She stayed much longer than the 48 hours she had planned, unable to drag herself away from her family and home. Under great pressure in the weeks before she came back and attending her two sister's weddings, she was reminded that her own marriage to Tom was only a distant possibility. She told her mother it had been so nice seeing them both again the day before she left and admitted she had been in two minds whether to return. 'You are such saints to me & I had such a nice time I don't feel at all like going back.' She was no longer eager and excited about returning to the Front, but she knew she could not stay at home because she would only be helping in the hospital where there was already sufficient staff. Torn as she may have been, there was really no choice for Dorothie. In Flanders she knew what she had to face; more deaths, the wounded, no hope of the war coming to an end soon, but she knew she could be more useful there. Her sense of duty and service towards those men who did not have the chance to go on leave and who faced danger, injury, and death most days made her go back. 'I got to love my soldiers like children.' She could not break their faith.

Dorothie finally went back in March but 'missed the dam boat' making her absence even longer. It is not clear whether she needed permission to take leave and was allowed a certain number of days. She may have taken the extra days and hoped to get away with it, but her extended absence had caused problems. Munro had not received a letter she had sent him explaining her delay, so the Mission had told Hély d'Oissel that she would not be coming back, and he had written to Dorothie 'in an awful stew'. Small details, time wasting and very aggravating; she was cross and decided she had to leave a card at the Mission to announce her return.

It took her until 17 March to find time to write home. 'Thank God I've got an armchair & a fire & a few minutes peace – Things have been an awful scrum since I got back.' New rules had been drawn up by the allies relating to English subjects working near the lines and on 19 March the hospital and the Corps thought they would have to drop out or officially join the Red Cross. This did not please Dorothie as it meant they would all be relegated to Boulogne or 'some Godforsaken spot'. Fortunately, the Belgians, including 'Papa' Broqueville, supported the Corps and hospital, so 'the clouds have cleared & we are now OK'. Dorothie believed what was needed for future use was a chit from the English Red Cross stating 'we are respectable people – & very nice too'. These problems were a constant trial to Dorothie and the severe emotional stress was not conducive to her general health.

On occasions, Dorothie suffered quite badly from period pains, which she referred to as 'Tonks', that sometimes obliged her to take to her bed. On 22 March she was forced to stay in bed as 'my dear friendly Tonks has occupied me with zeal that I couldn't stand any more'. Another cause could be that in times of stress periods often cease and, with Dorothie's idiosyncratic dietary habits, it may have caused her to suffer in this way. This time she felt worse than normal because although Dorothie was not a woman to give in easily to discomfort, she was also suffering from a chill, which made her feel even more ill.

Dorothy was unwell, and disheartened by the monotony and the inefficiencies of the war. This was compounded by some disquieting news about Tom Brockholes, the young man she hoped to marry and who meant so much to her. He had been wounded at the Battle of Neuve Chapelle (10-13 March) and she assumed he was not badly wounded, or she would have been informed. She had obtained the 'endless list' of casualties and deaths and thanked God that her brother Rollo had not been involved. To her it sounded a mess.

Our gunners fired a good deal on our own men & 3 times when they were supposed to have cleared the ground & the wire entanglements for an attack shot to shot with the result that our men rushed right up to the entanglements before they found they weren't swept away & had to retire losing a terrible amount of men in the retreat from the German fire – It's a ghastly thing anyway.

[22 March 2015]

Thinking of Tom Brockholes reminded her that her brother Hugh was on board the *Defence* bound for the Dardanelles. She asked her mother if there was any news.

When Dorothie received word about Tom it was devastating.

In the battle his battalion had been given a leading part in the attack, and was first to through the village on 10 March and entrench themselves on the far side. Two days later he was shot through the head while directing the fire of a machine gun in beating off a violent counter-attack, and died 14 March without recovering consciousness.

[De Ruvigney's Roll of Honour, 1914-1924]

The announcement of his injury was two weeks old when she heard that he was dead. To make it worse her mother's letters came in the wrong order and in the one she replied to, she had upset her mother by her uncaring response. When she did hear, she had been at dinner with a crowd and the shock was 'ghastly'.

As if this was not enough to bear, she then heard that Marjie's husband had been passed fit and would be going to the Front and that her father was sailing to Alexandria. Her mother would then be without all her family at Newnham. Peter was also going to the Front and Dorothie wrote again to castigate herself for being 'an utter pig' and for making it harder for her mother.

I am so so sorry I hurt you by my letter mother darling – I wrote it blindly & at the moment I couldn't understand your writing so casually that was all – Please forgive me & say a little prayer for me – Everyone is losing their bravest & their best & I suppose we must try & remember that – Poor Col Bridges boy .... was killed at Neuve Cap. too. It's awfully hard isn't it to remember the good side of this war, it's so easy for the women folk to see nothing but the misery of it all – & it's hard to be a patriot sometimes.

[3 April 1915]

Dorothie had plummeted to the depths of despair. Within the first six months of the war, she had lost Rupert Ommaney, one of her close friends, and now Tom, the man she loved. And her mother had to carry on running the hospital at home, lonely without most of her family, whilst her husband, her three sons and her daughter were actively involved in the war.

Dorothie did not mention Tom again in her letters until she finally left Flanders, but she was deeply affected by his death. She told her father about a ghastly morning on 23 March when people were blown to smithereens, and lots were wounded. Munro had left for England but the corps 'were going on just the same, with him and the Belgians and the Mission both said we may go on just the same as ever – that is to say the <u>women</u>'.

Thank God for that anyway – I just don't know what I should have done just now if I had had to check the active job & go & sit at home & twiddle one's thumbs – I honestly don't think I could bear it & ever so grateful that for the present at any rate the Mission (English) will sanction my working on the ambulances ... Oh Father why is this devilish war going on – It's so awful.

[25 March 1915]

Dorothie was at her most vulnerable at this point. During her the months at the Front she had seen so many deaths and injuries that she had become used to the constant stream of suffering. She cared about them, but she quickly had to learn to create a barrier to distance herself from the pain and suffering. On a few occasions an incident broke through and affected her deeply, especially at this vulnerable time. No doubt she was thinking of the wife and mother of a young Zouave soldier she had brought from Nieuport Bains to the hospital, and her recent bereavement made her more than usually sympathetic towards his family:

> He was dying but quite conscious & so plucky & talked to me so much about his home in Algiers – & his wife who he had married just before the war that he was mad about – He gave me her name and address & asked me to write her which I am doing to day as the poor kid died quite soon after getting to the hospital.

Dorothie witnessed many deaths, and on many occasions rushed to write to her mother – rarely checking for spelling and using a light, apparently carefree tone sometimes to disguise her grief – but not always.

Flanders 1915

War

A little cottage in a Flemish town, whitewashed outside & its rather dark rooms lighted up with flowers – Yes! flowers! – Lots & lots of them, poppies & purple thistles, cornflowers, great lilies & roses – from the hedges & fields & from deserted chateaux with poor gardens all smothered in shell holes – for in war I thirst for beauty in any shape or form – there is so much ugliness & squalor which somehow I never seem to get accustomed to – & flowers mean more to me now out here than I should ever have believed.

A wonderful sunset to-night, day is changing imperceptibly into night as the car glides softly down a tortuous road alongside the canal, which has caught the last reflections of the suns copper glory in her waters – The irregular warm toned roofs detach themselves in queer ghoulish shapes against the clouds, which are half hiding the moon to-night.

An evening meant for loveliness & peace.

A little 'poste de Secours' in the firing line near Dixmude, which in some miraculous way has escaped every shell for many months & remains deserted but untouched, the one solitary intact little homestead at the crossing of the roads.

A doctor opens the door, & the draught nearly upsets his candle although its light is shaded by a rolled up overcoat, for no lights must be shown.

A telephone rings sharply as I close the rickety door after me – it is the Colonel to say will we wait for a wounded man just been brought down from the outpost where he was hit by a shell early in the day.

A private in his Company sitting on the floor in the corner in the dark says 'Oui – c'est Jean – un brave – et le plus chic de notre compagnie – Il est mal arrangé pauvre diable, et blessés Dijon depuis 5 ou 6 heures mais ou n'as pa su l'apporter des avant posts avant la nuit. Il a 3 petits enfants lá bas á Liege

A shuffling of feet & a whispering outside the door, & a low moan – It is Jean Lafond – they were right – 'C'est un brave' – not a word of complaint, just a shuddering sigh as we put cushions & rungs round his poor shattered body & lift him oh! so gently onto the car.

As I am closing the curtains, there is a touch on my arm – It is one of Jean's comrades that helped to bring him in, & I see by the moonlight the pity in his eyes – 'Let me say goodbye to him' he whispers as he climbs in with a 'Bon Courage' before vanishing back into the night.

A long white road with a devilishly rough surface for a wounded man, but the moon to make amends comes out again, & together with the flares from the lines of the trenches on the left, helps to show up the holes, old & new with which this bit of road, (shell swept for many months) is pocket marked & scarred – The car jolts & creaks & that haunting crooning moan inside goes on to show that War & Death are taking as their toll a man who 6 hours ago was so alive & strong. Here is another harvest for them, another poor shattered body rendered almost unrecognisable

Pale face & ashen lips, & poor trembling frame. Why didn't Death gather you up in her strong arms – swift & almost tenderly as she does to some. Those are not to be pitied for they are beyond the barrier marking all suffering & pain, & there is no terror or horror in their eyes.

A little lantern flickering on the hospital gate, as we grope our way in – the stretcher is lifted down. There is no need to tire him further or even dress his wounds poor soul – he has not far to go now or much time left & we let him be.

The chaplain bends over him, one hears 'Je' sus' & that is all except that awful moaning has ceased – & I am so glad, Yes, glad, glad, glad, for if I too am to pass that way, I should thank God if he saw what the future held & saved me from it.

That is all – except that after the war – perhaps in a year or more, a woman at Liège will receive an intimation from the military authorities saying that 'Lafond, Jean – 1er Chasseaurs –

3eme Battaillon 2nd Compagnie est mort au champs de bataille le 26 Juin 1915 – prés de Dixmude; en faisant son ??? et en donnant á tous le plus bel example de bravoure'.

[In pencil]
PS
– Since I wrote this the little white home at the cross-roads has been shelled to pieces.

Dorothie knew her demeanour was causing concern and was full of praise for the English Mission who

… have been bricks to me & I won't have it said they aren't – They have also given me official permission to stay out here now & say they will no longer oppose it in any way & have written to Red X to say so – Bless them. I don't think you realise a bit what it would mean to me to not have a job now I nearly chucked it last week as I was so afraid I was blocking the work & I told the Mission I would leave it to them to decide – Johnie was perfect brick & has made everything allright & I am so grateful to him & always will be.

[2 April 1915]

Johnie Baird in British Counterintelligence was carrying out his duties as her godfather and a family friend in looking after Dorothie (insofar as that was possible), for which her family must have been very grateful, particularly her mother.

Focussing on work gave her the chance to get away from her thoughts, and there was plenty to do. From the beginning of

April there was an increase in military activity around Furnes and Dixmuide and on the last night of March Dorothie went looking for wounded. 'Such a gorgeous night … magnificent moon like day … It was very ghostly & gouly there in the moonlight.' The Germans were very close – right up the bridge on the other side of the river 25 yards across and Dorothie did not think they could be moved. The English lines were also very close. Most of the civilians were 'doing a bunk now'; probably fearing an attack, but Dorothie looked on the positive side and wrote that they would now have all the eggs, milk, and things they needed instead of having to 'nick' them. But she was still deeply affected by her personal losses and closed her letter with 'This is a damnable war – I wish I had been invented last generation.'

She described to her mother a typical day:

Our days work at present is (this is Jelly & my car) at 11.30 am we go to Nieuport Bains for Zouaves or Nieuport Ville for Marins, & nearly always bad cases then as that's in the town they shell most – We often take the bad cases down to a big French hospital near Dunkerque & it takes so long we don't get back to Furnes till 3 or so – Then do a Belgian round by Ramscappelle & Pervyse & in the evening after dinner go out to Kaaskerke, just again Dixmude, because at 9 o'clock the troops are changed & there are very often some blessés – If so by the time we take them to our hospital at Hoogstaat & get to bed its 12 or 1 o'clock.

Since Munro went is it so nice & peaceful for me – I let Bevan do all the dirty work & ordering & interviewing & seeing to things while I just fire away & hunt blessés which is the job I like & not hanging around the yard being plagued with people & things.

[10 April 2015]

Another way of distracting herself was collecting flowers to arrange in the house, and her sense of humour, which must have helped to keep her from deep despair, was never far from the surface.

I've got a lovely bunch of daffies in front of me as I write …. such nice big fat ones and I got a lovely bunch of peach blossom at Ramscappelle 3 days ago – I few minutes before I got there an obus has made an 'orrid hole in the garden but digging in the debris I found some violets & lots of peach blossom – something is so nice about finding flowers growing in spite of all the beastliness of shells & war. I enclose you a little bit –

The soldiers had put a chocolate cream – a great luxury – to set outside the door & the aforesaid 'obus' broke all the windows – covered them with mud but what was far worse put some hicks & a huge sod right into the pudding.

[10 April]

The next day Dorothie assured her mother she was still alive despite the heavy shelling in Furnes that morning. There was little damage, just a couple of blessés. In the afternoon aeroplanes dropped bombs, killing and wounding people just outside the house. She was rather cross with the local people who had collected about 300 stones to make a nice mark and sat 'to gape & watch the aeroplanes – then have a grievance when a bomb dropped in the middle of the bunch'. Colonel

Bridges, a friend who had just lost his son, was wounded, but as Dorothie described, not very badly. 'One piece through his cheek & jaw, small which they got out & a piece in his shoulder'.

The German army was obviously increasing the number of attacks and Dorothie reported that Furnes was being shelled and bombed every day. The hospital was hit and two of the Corps' cars were only saved from serious damage by a wall taking the shock. The Grande Place was riddled but none of the fine old buildings were hit, although all the glass was broken.

Yesterday we were lucky & only had about 5 blessés – one old gendarme had taken refuge in a cellar off the grande place & was wounded in it in spite of it & I am afraid very badly too – Dr. Jellett & I had an awful time getting him out & into the ambulance.

That really is very gruesome, that going round the town looking for poor devils that have been blesséd – & it's often not very plain sailing either as you never know when the next one is lumping in & whether at you or not – Dr. Jellett had one jolly close to him yesterday that way & Cooper had a brick that bruised his back a bit – I just hate this Furnes shelling – Much more than anything else.

No one was out of danger. Dorothie was startled to realise that the Germans seemed to know what was going on behind the Belgian lines and took appropriate action. Poincaré, the French Prime Minister, came to Nieuwpoort to visit General Hély d'Oissel. The Germans fired a 'french shell they had taken at Mantage, took the fuse out so it should arrive intact, & cut on it with a file, a verse to Poincaré asking him to accept the enclosed as an Easter Egg'. It arrived in time for him to receive it. Hély d'Oissel reported to Dorothie while the president and he were looking round, the Germans started shelling Poincaré's car. They were all fortunate to escape any injury.

More bad news about her family added to Dorothie's distress. Her cousin Edie Moore had died.

> I just can't believe it about Edie – one gets sort of numbed somehow & loses the power of realising that people have dropped out of ones life, there are so many horrors in this war ... She had such a fine soul & moral character it was always so hard her life should have been sort of wasted. Edie was capable of great things & would have done them too had chance put them in her way ... Poor little Edie – Its horrible somehow – Perhaps she has found her 'babies in heaven' & peace & her hearts desire & is perhaps happier now than before – If not I don't believe in heaven any more! If it isn't to cure all the heart aches of this world what's it for?
>
> [16 April 1915]

With the increasing number of deaths of loved ones Dorothie was struggling to reconcile her faith in the afterlife, and her prayers were obviously not giving her peace of mind.

There was little peace in Furnes, which continued to be bombarded, the shells and bombs coming over most days, and the Germans were also getting more accurate:

One nearly pipped me 3 days ago & still have a grievance – I was changing & greasing a wheel on the old ambulance outside our house door (not the hospital) in the street when dropped a bomb alongside. Breaks all the bedroom windows (mine included) throws a lot of mud on the bed & fills my throat & eyes with black smoke & beastliness & smothered the car with glass & debris.

[16 April 1915]

Dorothie was aware that there was a battle about to commence and in the frantic build-up she reflected on her home and family:

Are all the daffies out at home now? I find a few tired & sad looking ones in the deserted gardens at Nieuport, but they are nice nevertheless only they make me rather homesick & long for a look up the green avenue with the daffies dancing in the sunlight & nice clean grass & blow grow through you.

Tell me how they are this year please. I'd give a lot to see them & sit on the grass with the family & the tykes & all.

For a few days after this Dorothie had no time to write letters. The Second Battle of Ypres was about to start and was fought from 21 April-25 May 1915 to gain control of the strategic Flemish town of Ypres. It marked the first mass use by Germany of poison gas on the Western Front.

We have been terribly busy here these last four days – These dashed Germens advanced in a big fat slice between Steenstaade & Ypres made a hole through the French & Canadian divisions – took pots of prisoners & altogether did a far sight too well – We are now busy trying to counter attack & take it back, but beyond losing vast numbers of blessés & men there is no result. Its & bad business & was due to the French being knocked out 1st by asphyxiating shells & then the trenches carried – The Canadians I am told did splendidly – Glad to say it's not Hély d'Oissels division, but the officer Army Corps that gave way, let them through – The casualties are an average of at least 250 a day. <u>Monday</u> we work all night & day – Yesterday got to bed at 8 a.m – Im so tired – its beastly these days – Such crowds of wounded – poor poor souls – Last night was ghastly too out in a farm – Cannot write now.

[25 April]

She scribbled other letters in the half dark in the ambulance, on stand-by in case it was wanted. She felt it was the limit that Dunkerque had been bombarded with a big naval gun. She assessed it would be hard to put out of action as it was in a pit that gave it tremendous protection, but everybody was hoping for the best.

Dorothie knew that she was exhausted and took a few hours to try to recover.

I am lying on my underneath (dam uncomfortable too) in the sand by the sea, snatching a little peace – I am fed up with the war and very weary – We really have been very rushed lately & so many late nights make one rather tired – More so mentally than physically & I find myself getting very peevish & stuffy.

It must be 3 weeks now since we got to bed before 2 or 3 in the morning & many nights later – Yesterday we were at

Steenstraade till 5 am as there were a lot of wounded – French infantry mostly & you can only get then in at night – otherwise things have been quieter down there (danke gott) – Last night we got to bed at 12 till 3.30 am & then had to climb out because there was a call for a car & then turned in from 6 to 10 am again.

[1 May 1915]

Despite being exhausted and moody, she never failed to appreciate the beauty that sometimes took her attention from the horrors and stresses of war: 'One of the most lovely sights I have seen was 2 mornings ago dawn at Reninghe over the inundations, & to see the sun streaming up & being caught by the reflections in the waters & the ruined churches & villages sticking up out of it all.'

Meanwhile the battle was taking its toll.

Hely d'Oissel sent 2000 of his Zouaves down to reinforce the asphyxiated French at Lizerne & it was then they did that very fine attack & took the village but they lost 800 men out of 2000, a huge total & all except a tiny handful of officers – They have a wonderful fine 'moral' those Zouaves though of course it depends on lot on individual regiments – Many of the last turned out regiments are more hotel proprietors from Dinard than Algerians.

One Zouave was given the V C & made a Corporal lately for doing fine things & he told his Colonel he was afraid he wouldn't be much use as a Corporal as he could neither read or write – His Col told him not to fret as it was fighting wanted.

Hély d'Oissel saw this same tommy in hospital yesterday – He had been shot though both eyes (stone blind) in the attack at Lizerne & in awful pain but he never complained but said 'My General, you should tell the Colonel that he was right and it doesnt matter now that I know not how to read nor write.' I think its so sad.

Perhaps all these little things don't interest you – but its little trifles of pluck & all the millions of individual efforts that count in this war – The things that do one so much good too & make up for any nights up is the extraordinary gratitude of these men one helps. There are so many of them that think of such pathetic ways to thank you that it gives you a lump in your throat & makes one see red & want to put all these beastly Germans in pit & chop them up with spades like the boys used to do with jelly fish at Colwyn bay.

[4 May 1915]

The battle continued and Dorothie was kept very busy despite some days of calm. She wrote one letter in a dugout where an attack was going on by the Germans – Dorothie complained that they had started five hours too early. Every gun was being fired and the road was impassable, so any rescues were impossible. Later she noticed relief troops going up the road and was frustrated because she did not know what was going on. There was a great deal of artillery activity and Dorothy and Dr Jellett were kept busy sharing the driving of 'Daniel', their ambulance. Dorothie described yet another of her near misses:

Yesterday it really was rather unpleasant & it's amazing how the Almighty looks after our crowd – I was driving down an open

French Zouaves in camp between the dykes.

The extraordinary effect of artillery over time; the remains of Ypres in the snow.

bit of canal and (the one I had a nightmare about one night I was sleeping with Mrs Ma) & they amused themselves by having pots at us as we went by – & one was bang in front of the car on the road & for the life of me I don't know why we didn't meet any of the bits – I could hardly see either where the road was to steer straight as there was a good deal of dust & smoke.

[9 May 1915]

It was relentless. The Germans fired 25,000 shells in the Nieuwpoort area and the allies fired 1,000 back, creating the most deafening noise. They were bursting continuously, and it must have looked like a scene from hell. Little harm was done, and Dorothie would have considered it a complete waste of time and money.

Dorothie was not recovering her former good health. She was beginning to get the jumps as she was feeling 'rather cheap & backachy & "wish I was dead" sort of thing' so gave herself 24 hours off, and the rest did her good. She was also given a break by the arrival of Robert de Broqueville who arrived in Furnes to carry her off for the night to the chateau where his father was staying.

Its a charming little old chateau with pretty grounds & a weedy avenue full of buttercups & all so peaceful – nice the war seems years away – Its a most pleasant place & I shall come for a day whenever fed up with life – the war or the Munro Corps – Its nice to be in a strange bed & away from the same old faces for a change – I'd give a lot for 3 days at N P [Newnham Paddox] on my back in the grass with nothing to do!

[14 May 1915]

On 17 May she was back in Furnes and despite the continuing battle it was quieter in the area, and she was able to invite the Admiral to dinner. Her concern at that stage was shortage of money and she asked her mother to send her some towards her keep as all she had 'in the world today is 1/6 in German money that belonged to a German before last Sunday's attack'.

She and Dr Jellett were the only occupants of the house as all the other members had gone home on leave, and Dorothie found it much more to her liking as it was somewhere quiet to return to after a day's work. As it was a bit large for both of them, she decided she would contribute to the running expenses and as she was responsible for the housekeeping, she also asked for refugee contributions. She had taken time to write this after being 'smothered in oil & am just scrawling this after having had a full morning filling grease caps on the old ambulance.' She managed to enjoy a ride on the sands: 'Pierre de Broqueville in cavalry (Robert's brother) is quartered up the road these days & lends me a gee – Had a beauty yesterday – It is lovely to get a real ride & some eccer – & now the evenings are long I can often have one between tea time when we come in & before going out again at 9 pm'.

Dorothie was still suffering from depression.

I wish to God we were all home again – Its so very very dreary sometimes though one pretends it isn't – Its a year but two months since I left home for the old Rugby Hospital – a big slice you know – & I've had a slackers time compared to poor Tubby so heaven knows how sick they must get of it & as for you – it makes my heart ache – Poor mother – I do wish I could do something to make things easier for you – I write as often as I can & will write oftener – Thank you so much for all your nice letters – they are so nice you can't think – Theres hardly any evening I come in without something from home.

[18 May 1915]

Other concerns were raised over gossip: 'It appears bally Belgians & dirty dogs have been spreading yarns that I had no business to be there alone with Jellett.' She was keen to inform her mother that there was no alternative and that Bevan had asked the Mission advice about the 'lady question'. They were very indignant and told him to pay no attention and that it did not matter a scrap. Dorothie knew her mother would understand the situation and that Dorothie's reputation would not be compromised by Dr Jellett – she knew her daughter's thoughts on men very well – nevertheless, Dorothie wanted to pre-empt gossip and had to use her precious spare moments to find another female lodger.

I will try to arrange if possible later for Mrs Wynne & I to dig together but at present as she & Bevan do Coxyde, & the night trip there, they have to sleep down near on account of late calls & being on the spot – She is in the same quandary – So what I am doing is, getting in Hélène our refugee girl that used anyhow to be at home all day to sleep there as well & if possible will get some other members of the Corps shortly to come too – The Coopers & co cant as they are probably going down nearer Ypres with a small unit of our cars – But anyway I will do my best to get some more members in – not that we would see anything of them as we are out from shortly after breakfast to anything up to 3 a m! – I am just writing to you all this in case you might get yarns via Dunkerque or some busy body which would worry you, whereas there is nothing to be worried about when you know the facts – Jelly is a hot tempered old cuss but a very good sort really & does his work A1 – & is one of the most genuinely useful members we have in the Corps.

[22 May 1915]

The countess was far more worried about her daughter's health. Aware of this Dorothie promised to send her a daily card to reassure her that she was still going strong. But her mother was insistent and wanted her home and was so concerned she offered to pay Dorothie's fare. Dorothie explained there were various reasons why she would rather leave it a few weeks:

I am afraid you are thinking I am tired out? – Its not so & this last week has been one of the quietest just in our district that I have known for some time – & I am not a bit hard worked for the moment.

Next week too, Boches permitting I mean to take 3 days absolute peace at Broquevilles chateau. I think the Corps will be undergoing some radical change very shortly & we are in the midst of various negotiations with the authorities – So I do not want to go away till that is settled – If I came home now I would probably only have to dash back & I would much rather come home for a longer while a little later when things are settled.

[25 May 1915]

By 25 May, the Battle of Ypres was over. Official records counted 80,000 casualties, thousands of whom had been rescued by Dorothie and her colleagues. The outcome was that the Ypres Salient had been compressed and Ypres itself was closer to the line. Dorothie was waiting for the final settlement of the Monro Corps; Mrs Knocker & Mairi Chisolm decided to leave the corps and set up their own dressing station five miles east in a town named Pervijze, north of Ypres, just one hundred yards from the trenches. Here, in a vacant cellar which they named 'Poste de Secours Anglais' (British First Aid Post), the two would spend the next three-and-a-half years tending to the wounded. and Sarah McNaughton had gone home to lecture 'on the perils of war' (she has never been near!). The Corps was changing, and this was why there was only Jellett and herself at No. 14. Now it was officially settled, she went home on leave.

The countess's visit in early December had been a time of great joy, but Dorothie's mother had also seen the terrible conditions in the hospital and that many of the soldiers needed respite before they returned to the Front, which was impossible as there were no facilities in the area. Being a practical woman, she offered Newnham Paddox as a convalescent home and the first soldiers arrived in later December, escorted by Elsie Knocker, who was going home on leave. The countess was shocked when she saw them as she was expecting 'sitting or walking cases who could benefit from the lovely grounds'. Instead, she was faced with stretcher cases 'two head wounds, one amputated leg, two men with serious abdominal complications, and one with a horribly fractured thigh'. Dorothie had intended to tell her mother about their condition before they arrived. They had been sent to Hôpital IV, a French military hospital in Zuydcoote, near Dunkirk, where Dorothie's sister Marjie was a nurse. They were to wait until arrangements had been made, but the doctor refused to keep them as he had more serious cases coming in. Dorothie asked her mother to forgive such short notice – 'but that is the worst of war'.

Not only was the countess involved but so, too, were local people in the village. Ever brisk and single-minded, Dorothie made assumptions about other people's reactions without consulting them. She prayed that 'the neighbours would (also) forgive such short notice. I feel they will be glad to have 'blessés' & glad to have some real nursing to do as a result of all the Red X lectures & work they have done' and as these people had subscribed locally to the war, she thought it 'would please them to have a finger in the pie & the looking after the actual blessés'.

5

RATHER A RAG LATELY, BACK ACHES & THINGS

Dorothie returned to Flanders in late June, accompanied by another dog, her small terrier Charles, who was to bring her great joy. The leave had done her a great deal of good:

> It has been so nice at home & such a wonderful rest morally as well as physically – I feel I could strangle millions of Huns now all on my lonesome ... You have been so sweet to me mother, thank you with all my heart ... thank you so much – & not only for that but for all your love & sympathy to me while I was home – You can't imagine the good it did me – The moral change & rest more than anything & how much better I feel for it.
>
> [18 June 1915]

Although the countess had no fears about her daughter's morals, she was no doubt pleased that the refugee girl,

Hélène Van de Wende, had moved into No. 14. Although a servant she would provide some female company for Dorothie and taking over the household chores from her would leave Dorothie with more time. 'Another girl who moved in was called Zenobie who was also a refugee. Gave them a home, servants, security, wages.'

The situation in Flanders was still stalemate.

Last night I got to bed at 4.30 a m & they started shelling Furnes at 6. Not much peace & close to our home which is tiresome of them. One bang frightened poor wee Charles to death & he hid his head & fore paws under the pot stand – & imagined himself quite safe! – He makes me laugh. Dunkirk has been badly potted again to-day too – 1st time for a month –

Situation is unchanged all along here. No advance to speak of anywhere.

[22 June 1915]

Although Dorothie had enjoyed her leave she was able to think objectively about where she would rather be and, despite the home comforts and her time with her mother, her sister Squeaker and the 'stugs', Dorothie's pet name for the children, she had no doubt that Flanders was the right place for her.

Its so odd to be back in the same old place doing the same old things – some old obus, same old faces, same old late nights, same old everything, – It's a very nice thought to be doing something & entirely a degree of hate – I hated going away from home & coming back, but I should hate far more to have nothing to do at home, so have no grievance at all really – Each time one gets the joy of a real good lay at home & is tempted perhaps to chuck things up, one realises its only because its temporary that 'bath mats' are so very pleasant – & of all the jobs going in war time I think I have the best. Perhaps hard in some ways, but it is most extraordinarily interesting being right at the heart & pulse of things & feeling you count & can help a great deal – An indoor hospital life at Balham would be like a general who is 'dégummé' as the French say, shellshocked & sent to run transport at a base in Lands End – Just as useful no doubt, but how dull oh Lord how dull!

I'd rather be obussed any day.

[30 June 1915]

It had been a fortunate decision to take Charles the terrier back with her. He provided Dorothie with a means of distraction from her anxieties and the persistent stress. Charles was a source of constant entertainment and life was 'full of excitement with him about'. Dorothie regularly entertained her family with reports of his activities. He was frequently flea-bitten, had constant skin problems, suffered from fits following which he was sick in various places, rolled in 'something perfectly appalling' such as a six-month-old ham which he had dug up, became involved in fights with other dogs (which he usually started) or chased cats. He also stole food from No 14 and from nearby neighbours. Despite all these crimes he was 'a dear and the joy of my life –it was a real brainwave to bring him'. Whether the inhabitants of Furnes were as enamoured of him is not recorded, but the soldiers loved him unreservedly because he belonged to 'Mees'. They were continually rescuing him from dangerous situations or searching for him when he went missing, to mutual amusement.

And the war went on relentlessly. On the last of day of June, the Germans started to shell the French Headquarters and five of the Marins were killed. Dorothie went to see if there were any wounded, but they had been killed instantaneously and were 'terribly smashed'. She observed, 'It's never so bad though when you know people have been killed absolutely like that. They are ones Death is kindest to.' Dorothie saw horrendous injuries most days and she could say with stark candour that often death was the kindest outcome. She saw many deaths and was moved by them all, but one or two affected her deeply and produced some of her finest writing. Death could be a better answer than suffering.

Dorothie witnessed these and other scenes nightly – 'Since I left Newnham, we turned in every night between 1. Am & four am' – and explained how difficult it was to get the wounded to hospital.

The troops aren't relieved till 11 pm sometimes later now, its so late, then there have been a lot of blessés among the outposts all the Dixmude way, as the Belgees & Huns are at places amazingly near (25 yds) (for Belgees!) & it takes a terribly long time to get them in – Last night up there 2 brancardiers started at 10 pm to fetch a wounded man from the outposts & only got him back at ten am next morning – There is some miles of very exposed communication trench, cut zig zag of course with the result no stretcher can be taken in it & the blessé has to be slung in his blanket & carried by the other men on all fours.

[1 July 1915]

As well as physical injuries Dorothie had to deal with men who were mentally disturbed.

> Yesterday we had an awful time with a tame Zouave lunatic they very kindly gave 'Mees' at Nieuport to take away – He was just cheerfully balmy, rather like Neb when tight, & was very funny – He had hotly accused his Lieutenant of having cut his wife into little bits with his scissors, which just gave his bright pals the idea he might be queer – wonderful how observant men get you know – So the patient alternatively took me for the lieutenant, the wife, the scissors, his best friend & something most unpleasant – & kept trying to climb out at the back when we weren't looking.

There were compensations, times of relief from the relentless work. One evening during the ceaseless travelling back and forth to rescue the wounded, Hély d'Oissel 'carried me off to dine with him' and she was delighted by a kind action from Commandant Paillet, whom she described as 'a funny old boy, 2nd in command of the Marins & he found me looting roses in Nieuport – He's rather a wag, & fled down to his office in a cellar & made me out the enclosed 'bon' with the freedom to loot Nieuport!!!'

Hely d'Oissel invited her to dine about every ten days and she looked forward to these evenings with much pleasure. 'It does me good to get away from everything.' He probably looked forward with as much pleasure to her company. She was a delightful dinner guest, charming and witty, but undemanding. They would sit quietly together, the General writing his orders and Dorothie taking the opportunity to write home.

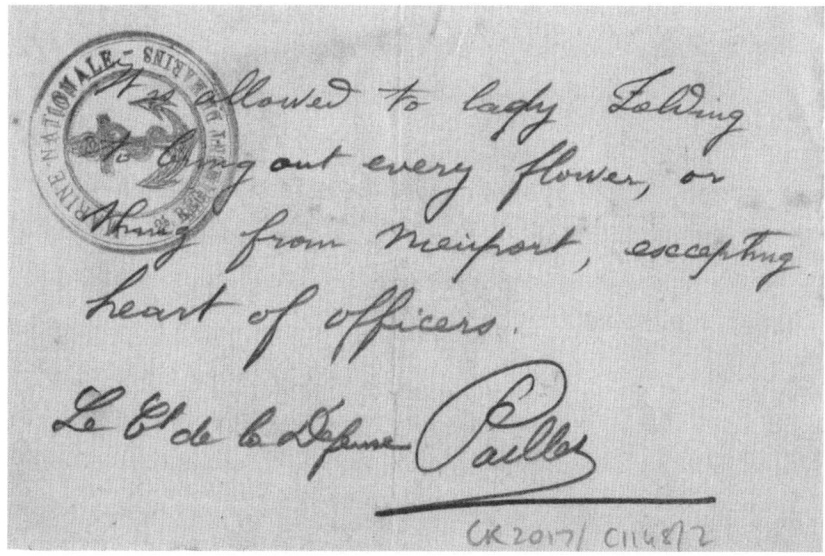

allowed to Lady Felding
...ing out every flower, or
...from Nieuport, excepting
heart of officers.
Le Cᵗ de la Défense — *Paillet*

CR 2017/ C11482

Letter from Commander Paillet allowing Dorothie to steal flowers!

Dorothie was immensely popular with all the soldiers and was particularly fond of the Zouaves, who adored her. On July 4 they asked her to a tea party which she said Hugh would have loved, as there were lots of drinks. She had been invited to be 'godmother' to the Marins' flag they had just made:

The dear fat old Col. of Zouaves was the godfather – I found to me horror on arriving at Oostdunkerque – about 1½ miles behind the lines at Nieuport Bains all the Zouave regimental band drawn up who played God Save the King & Tipperary & every sort of thing they could think of that had any connection with 'Mees' – Then Col. Roland made a speech of some ½ hr which made me hotter & hotter till I nearly fell thro' the floor in a puddle, & then I christened the 'fanion' & we drank buckets of champagne & ate hundreds of jam tarts till we felt sick as dogs – Then a concert, really quite good sung by lots of the tommies who are opera singers. They gave me a dashed fine Hun obus with flowers in it & all sorts of wonderful engravings on it done by the Zouaves & really very nice – a copper plate let into with my name & union jacks & Zouave monograms & red crosses, & auto-cannons – In fact every dam thing they could think of.

[4 July 1915]

Dorothie took great delight in spending frivolous times with the soldiers. But she also enjoyed telling a good tale in her letters and her tone of mock-embarrassment was part of her story-telling technique to amuse her readers at home. For both Dorothie and the soldiers, such apparently cheerful behaviour was a mechanism for coping with the tedium and misery of their situation.

It was not long before reality came back. Her mother told her that Peter, Dorothie's youngest brother, had been injured and was in hospital. An opportunity arose for her to visit Peter, but before she could go the Germans launched another attack that badly affected Nieuwpoort. Her skills were needed there.

They put 17 inch into Nieuport again last night absolutely buried about 20 men in the cellar of one of the houses – Some are still alive under it all poor devils or rather were last night – They have been working to move the debris for 12 hrs & haven't got down to them yet – The whole home crumpled up like a pack of cards. They are awful these 17 in – Like a train coming through the air.

Fortunately, she was able to visit Peter later, which cheered them both up. He was scabby but smiling and obviously recovering well. His wristwatch had been badly damaged, and Dorothie immediately suggested sending it to Squeaks for her museum.

Much worse news followed closely. François 'Floch' Hély d'Oisel, a relative of the General, had been killed in his aeroplane, having only just obtained his pilot's licence the week before: another young man for Dorothie to add to her list of dearly loved lost friends.

She was also under great stress from having to share the house with Dr Jellett, whom she sometimes found to be moody and intrusive. Unfortunately, in Dorothie's eyes, her mother was always concerned about Dorothie's health and had asked Jellett to keep an eye on her.

He responded:

Dear Lady Denbigh

I think Lady Dorothie is in very good health and stands the life here on the whole very well. I am however sometimes annoyed with her for not eating better because when she does not eat properly at one meal, she is rather inclined to want less at the next, and so on. A lecture from you in this matter would do her no harm, and also taking as much sleep as she can get …

We were in Ypres the other day and I found a very excellent tonic in a deserted chemists shop which I am trying to get here. I think it will do her a lot of good. I am going to make her go back for a week or two in August.

Dorothie appreciated her mother's concern but was irritated by Jellett's determined efforts to oversee her health.

About my health Mrs Ma, please don't worry, because honest injun if I was seedy I should tell you & Dr Jelly too – as I promised him I would – He is an awfully good old thing – & most extraordinarily kind to me in every kind of way. But when we are alone as we are now he is sometimes terribly 'tiring' – Being very Irish & rather rough, & very hot tempered, & worst of all very touchy. You know what I mean like gooys are sometimes & inclined to make mountains out of the tiniest molehills & take it for granted everyone finds fault with him – well when he does that (as he happens to be doing now!!!) it makes one awfully tired, because one never never gets a minute to oneself. You see when we were several, it didnt matter so much & one just loafed off until he recovered – whereas now sometimes when I am weary & feel if I saw old Dr Jelly another 5 minutes I should scream & go off to my room & just slack by myself & Charles with a book until I am fit to speak to again – So I think perhaps often when I go off like this that he thinks it's because I'm overtired & I cant very well say it's just because I must have a little bit of the day to myself or it makes me nervy – So you mustn't think I am seedy – until I say so – I am writing this to explain – & it's private of course – But old Jelly is so very kind & such a real good sort in every other way that it easily makes up for his irritations as everyone has their faults, & as he is older & very respectable as Mama would say, he is about the only member of the Corps I would dig with like this.

And I don't for a minute imagine I'm not a bit of a trial myself at times.

So there we are – Its all part of the discomforts – mental especially – that one has to take as the days work.

When Dorothie wrote to her father, she was more honest about her mental health. She had been feeling gloomy and wishing that she was dead but told him that his letter had made her feel better. She also confided in him that she was worried about her mother. When Dorothie had been on leave, she had thought that her mother was looking rather worn out and blamed it on the fact that she did too much work and sat writing endless letters until 2 or 3 o'clock in the morning. Dorothie was also dismayed that Squeaks was leaving to take up a Red Cross role, which would leave her mother with no family at home. Dorothie told him:

I wish this ghastly business was over – Even when it is over God knows what will be left to us – Its almost simpler for those that are blown up I think – Its easier than for those that are left with just a heartache – Its so late & I must go the bed I suppose.

I do wish I could come & see you for a little but & get away from all this beastliness & sorrow – It's the endlessness & futility of it that is so despairing.

[11 July 1915]

Dorothie also realised her mother was under stress. She wrote to sympathise and told her how sorry she felt for her 'poor Mrs Ma' and commiserated with her about Squeaks going away. She also enclosed some photos to 'amuse' her. But even though she always tried to allay her mother's fears, she often unthinkingly told her things that would add to her mother's concerns:

A big german offensive is expected & all along between Ypres & the sea end of Aug or Sept. In fact during the autumn – of course the poor old allies advance that was to take place in April is rather a frost! – But they say the germans having now set so effectively on the Russians are now bringing back huge quantities of the troops & guns for this Western offensive – Till then I think there won't be much doing – just the same steady fighting & endless casualties without either side getting any further – Oh La oh La.

[12 July 1915]

This offensive was to be known as the Battle of Loos, which began later that September, but such information must have been top secret and known only to those at top military

The British at the Battle of Loos, 1915. 'From what I can ascertain, some of the divisions did actually reach the enemy's trenches, for their bodies can now be seen on the barbed wire.' (General Rawlinson.)

Gas attack on the Hohenzollern Redoubt at Loos, October 1915. While the French went on the offensive in Champagne and Artois, the British fought at Loos.

level. Dorothie was clearly close to vital and secret sources of information. How had such an indiscreet letter got past the censor? Dorothie makes it clear in her letters that she objected to being censored and found ways to get her letters home without intervention. She often asked officers or other military personnel to take her letters back to England with them.

In her precious free moments Dorothie mood lightened and she found time to write longer letters on subjects unconnected with the war.

This home is too smart now & is getting very like Frankton – Has nifty curtains, (from ma) priceless furniture (Nieuport) wonderful gold rimmed dinner service (Ypres) & lovely brass –

copper & china antiques, (Flanders generally) hanging all round the walls.

And beautiful garden at the back with terrier in same – by name Charles, one hen by name Mabel, one rabbit by name Pierre.

In fact its really almost too nice & comfortable now – I think I'd never have the courage to go back to real war & real dirt & never taking off ones trowsers.

[13 July 1915]

She also asked for a cake – 'a nice stiff one with currants & weevils – we never lunch in but have a sandwich in the car & it's a luxury to have a cake in the house & I am too lazy & too busy to make one myself.' The countess was only too pleased to oblige, the cake arrived two days later. (Mail delivery to and from the Front was amazingly efficient.)

It was not only the death and injuries of soldiers that upset Dorothie. She had grown fond of the towns and villages where she worked, and the slow but gradual destruction of their buildings added to her melancholy. On the evening of 12 July, she and Jellett were:

Just off to our nightly round near Dixmude – There is a little white house at the X roads up to now a sort of mascot & untouched which has been used as a dressing station since Oct: & which we have been to I should be sorry to say how many times – I had a great affection for it as its 'luck' has often stood us in good stead, especially the 'Yser' days – To my sorrow two nights ago I rolled up as usual & found it a wreck, having been badly shelled that afternoon & again yesterday –

The dressing station is now a neighbouring dug-out & I weep salt tears over the ruins of our poor little house there whenever I see it – Luckily no one was hit in it as the 1st two shells fell short & gave them warning.

[13 July 1915]

Dorothie knew that the Germans were determined to smash the locks at Nieuwpoort so that the flooding could gradually subside, but as soon as they were damaged the engineers built them up again – yet another example of the lack of progress in that tedious war.

The weather conditions often added to the difficulties of fetching the wounded. In July the sunshine was interrupted by unseasonable rain.

Such a day & night yesterday – Howling gale & rain – I was soaked twice & swallowed a few ton of sand & mud in the dunes & on the roads in the course of the day – You cant think what those roads through the dunes are like in a storm – The sand simply beating down & the air full of it & it hurts your face so driving against it one can hardly steer – The night was black as ink, & of course it was skiddy & poor blessés in the car Dixmude way, & the road invisible.

[18 July 1915]

To comfort herself in these dire conditions she thought of being at home dressed in a red flannel jacket drinking a gin. There was no flannel jacket at No.14, but she did have a brown silk and wool jersey that her mother had sent, which delighted her and that she wore every morning. She may have worn it when she took Charles for a long walk by the canal. The weather had improved by 20 July and that evening there was a magnificent sunset with the the red roofs reflected in the water. The bright lights had turned everything to a copper gold. It brought back memories of the three days she had spent in Granada some years before and for a few hours the war seemed far away.

Dorothie went few places without her camera and in late July she and Jellett were in Pervyse and went to look at the cellar house, her old home. The cellar was 'all stove in now' and full of water, with no roof, and a child's cradle and red cotton umbrella floating in the dirty water.

It all looked so disconsolate I wanted to photograph it for you as it now is & you must thank that photograph when you get it for saving our lives. We had just stopped inside the doorway to do the photo when a clutch of four shells fell at intervals of 10 yds apart up the road we had just been standing on – Half a minute sooner & we simply wouldn't have helped being hit. A sentry who was standing there was killed poor soul – Dr Jelly was there & did what he could for him at once, but the main artery in his neck was cut & he died in a few minutes – If only he had had the tiniest chance of life, we might have made the whole difference being there, as our car was 100 yds off & we could have taken him right away – it was it was all very gruesome.

[20 July 1915]

Dorothie was used to the daily toll of soldiers and civilians, but this incident affected her deeply. Although she could accept death she could still not get used to its extraordinary swiftness. She questioned the existence the afterlife.

It takes someone like that a few yards from you & then perhaps in a few minutes you are right away in a new atmosphere & perfect safety & in different surroundings with people laughing & talking & it seems a century since one stood alongside Death.

But somehow out here the thought of it doesn't frighten me an atom as it would have in the old days – It just seems natural & one never thinks about it.

But it sometimes makes it very hard to believe in the existence of a future life, or rather the need for one – After all, people are alive one moment & cease to be the next & why should there be any kind of future? – When one sees Death in ones & twos in everyday life, there seems some sort of necessity for something further, but now that Death deals in hundreds & thousands, one thinks of people as being the same as any of Gods other creatures, & why we should have anything more than any of the other animals is hard to understand & honestly I dont understand.

[20 July 1915]

Dorothie never questioned her faith in God, nor his purpose for all mankind. It may be one reason why she took such tremendous risks, believing that she was carrying out her duties to help those who needed her help. If she died whilst doing so, it was the will of God. But to question one of the tenets of Catholic faith was surely a sign of deep despair.

She did not discuss this with Dr Jellett, who seemed unaware of her inner turmoil. However, the countess must have been extremely worried about Dorothie's state of mind and had written to Dr Jellett for his opinion, who, apparently, gave it:

I am glad to say I have no fault to find with your daughter.

Lady Dorothie is a charming girl, & eats for six – I fear she may grow too stout for the ambulance & I shall have to build an annexe – which would be fatiguing – I forgot to mention that Lady D is of an amiable disposition but rather disfigured at the moment by 3 mosquito bites on her clock.

Her dog Charles is covered in sulphur & train oil to cure him of that disgusting habit 'itchio magnificus' – So I have put them both to sleep in the outhouse for the moment with 'Pierre' the rabbit & 'Mabel' the hen. Believe me madam

Yrs sincerely

H Jellett – M.S. Vet. Surgeon

The countess would have immediately recognised her daughter's handwriting and realised this was meant to alleviate her fears. She may have been relieved about Dorothie's eating habits, but the concern over Dorothie's thoughts would not go away.

Dorothie did not allow her herself to wallow in despondency and one of the best ways of restoring her to a happier mood was dining with de Broqueville. Dorothie would have described him as 'one's own sort' and being with him she could relax, laugh and talk about subjects other than the war. And there was always some small, insignificant incident to make Dorothie smile:

One funny episode of the day was a Majors orderly who had gone out to get his C O fresh eggs & had put them in his trouser pocket for safety – Arrives an obus some 15 yds off – a little one, but enough to give the orderly a bad fright & he ducks madly, which of course broke all the eggs! A sitting position is not conducive to the safeguarding of a clutch of eggs in the trowser pouch!

It was very funny to see the orderlie's face of disgust when he diskivered the tragedy & to see the egg mess.

[21 July 1915]

In the same vein as these light-hearted moments was her 'wheeze' for going to see Rollo. She had met an old friend, Major Lumsden, who was based at Bethune, and she had invited him to dine with her. Dorothie was not one to miss an opportunity. She said that she felt it in her bones 'that if I ask him nicely he will aid and abet me getting down for another day' to see Rollo. It would have been a fait accompli – few could resist Dorothie's charm.

Some letters are very short! '27th July – Morning Mar – I love you – Havent time to write – How sad the swallows have gone – Yr loving Dodo – Aunt Mabel sent me 200 cigs – I love her P.S. Dear Countess – I love you – you love me?' Did Dorothie smoke? or were the cigarettes for the troops?

Her bones' prediction was accurate about Rollo (Tubby) but they kept two more surprises for her. 'Hurrah & Hurrah – I saw Tubby & Peter yesterday – Had a whole day down at Bethune thanks to the kindness of Major Lumsden – Both are as fit as fleas – I am mad with joy at Tubby getting that staff job.'

From deep despair Dorothie emotions rose to elation at the sight of two brothers and news of one's removal from the Front. Major Lumsden had done more than Dorothie had asked for, and she was very grateful.

> The kind man, sent his car all the way up here for me & sent me back at night also went to endless trouble collecting the 2 boys for lunch & the afternoon & hacking them back down the lines.
>
> Rollo smothered in swanking staff bands & full of bounce & looking too well for words – Honestly really & thoroughly well & in great spirits – Peter too with a hard scab left & full of smiles – He pottered about all the afternoon & Lumsden took us all to see the big Coventry 15 in howitzers he is in charge of – The shells are half as much again as the German 17 in ones they throw at us here & that bucked me up no end to think how we too must be fighting them in return.
>
> [26 July 1915]

After a delightful day she was sleepy and would rather have gone to bed, but instead she had to go to Dixmuide and reported that the Germans had shelled Furnes that night.

Others perhaps tried to keep Dorothie's mind away from brooding with silly pranks:

> The Admirals & young sparks – Young Ronarch & Deforge tried to pull my leg last night but it failed & I am a hen to the good (Named Alice) which is always something – The front door has a window over it – or rather had because one of the bombs broke the glass bien entendu, & the result is there is just a draught as I haven't been able to afford glass except for my bedroom.

Well they all turned up at 3 a m with a sack – & a cat & a hen in it – They squared the sentry at the X roads outside & climbed up & dropped the hen in, then the cat who had a long string & a tin box with shrapnel bullets in it to rattle & a caricature of me – They had carefully ascertained that Charles hated cats & of course expected him to be sleeping in the kitchen & to give chase & raise hell generally.

However Charles being in my bed room it fell flat because the cat escaped in the garden, leaving his tin box behind, & Hélène put the new hen in the pen with 'Mabel' the hen & 'Pierre' the rabbit – I heard a row but didn't bother, it seemed quite usual somehow to hear a hen on the landing & didn't interest me enough to get me out of bed – It teased old Jelly a bit as he got up in the dark & nearly fell downstairs & couldn't find the match or the hen.

[28 July 1915]

This sort of behaviour may seem trite and silly from two young men, soldiers, who were involved in a deadly war. But in such times people need a relief from the destruction going on around them and were probably aware that it could be one of them whose life would be lost, another name added to the thousands of the dead. Emotions are stretched to their limit and pranks such as these should be understood in this light. Dorothie, from the life with her brothers and their friends, was aware that young men acted like this even when they were at home. Her response was to invite them to supper.

But she could not always hold the sad thoughts at bay, and she kept returning to trying to come to terms with death.

Mother dear – I got your long dear letter last night for which many thanks – It was a help too because one's poor mind & judgement is rather inclined to get lost in the dark & inclined to chuck it up at times.

What I mean is, that although the war brings one closer to prayers & does not diminish ones faith as a Catholic in the smallest degree, it makes one rocky over the root principle of any after life at all – or rather the sadness & completeness of death so often & so very close to one, somehow does away with the whole theory of a future of any kind – Why should there be one? – There isn't any need for one any more than for any other animal – But I do believe the need of religion in a race – because it brings out all the noblest & the best morally, & individually stands for betterment & continuance of the whole race generally doesnt it. Therefore I think that even if there is no future existence at all, one has not right to squander ones life or things slide, or humanity as a whole would go to pot – See what I mean? – Its seeing Death in such numbers & such simplicity that makes me think this – Because somehow the fact of Death in the abstract has no 'Fear' now like it used to when one thought about it in the old days – But although still wanted to do the square thing on earth it doesnt seem to matter to the smallest degree what happens 'after' or if there is an after or not – It just doesn't matter anymore now some how – I think people just live & do their best & then die – & there an end of it – It seems so easy to believe in God but no need for heaven!

Dear me how complicated its all getting – I'd better leave it! Because after all I'm one in many millions & it don't really count or matter what I finks.

[30 July 1915]

Fortunately, after such soul-searching she went to dinner with
the General and her mother must have been overjoyed by her
daughter's suggestion of going home in August. The countess
sent Dorothie a cake and some tins of toffee, which cheered
Dorothie up and prompted her to reassure her mother that
Furnes was 'nice& peaceful', but that she and Jellett had
missed an opportunity of a decent supper.

> Rather sad I was done out of a hen for dinner – on the way into
> Nieuport we saw a decapitated hen lying on the road, whether
> by obus or motor I know not (but out of spirit I know) and
> done too; & asking to be picked up for the larder – only Jelly &
> I both were suffering from cold feet as they were shelling the
> road & the last 3 had been rather close – So we put our nose in
> the air & pretended we did not want it – However on the return
> journey we eagerly scanned every inch of the road, it being them
> so nice quiet – but a wily & braver looter had been there 1st &
> we went home henless after all – A bit 'ard – but will larn us to
> funk.
>
> [2 August 1915]

The countess knew with fearful certainty, and at frequent
cost to her peace of mind, that Dorothie would never funk
anything.

Dorothie added to the mother's pleasure by telling her she
was going to spend a couple of days at the Broqueville chateau.
Not for long! Typically, Dorothie told her mother that she had
ricked her back and that it was hurting a lot. The doctor had
checked it, and it seemed to be getting better, but Dorothie
was relieved not be to be bumping about in the ambulance in

and out of potholes all day. She had enjoyed two quiet days but although she said her back was much better, she intended to slack for the next few days. Her mother would have seen though this thin attempt to disguise the fact that the back was still troubling her. Slacking was also something that Dorothie would never do, unless there was a very good reason. Still, on occasions she committed other offences: 'I've just stolen armful of flowers to take back with me – In fact was so ashamed of the quantity & the gardener's wrath that I wrapped them up in a rug & pretended it was "only a corpse".' Desperate to have flowers, for once she forgot her manners in omitting to ask permission.

Back at No. 14, Dr Jellett checked Dorothie over and found nothing except an intermittent pulse. He suggested that she should not worry about it, but he would not let her go out at nights. He was worried but kept his concerns to himself for the moment.

Her mother and father must have been extremely proud to hear that Dorothie had received another medal. Typically, Dorothie told her mother about the activities of her rabbits and recounted Charles' frequent misdeeds before informing her mother in a postscript:

I quite forgot to tell you the Admiral presented me with the french 'Croix de Guerre' two days ago – It is the order just been issued for all who have been mentioned in despatches – The Admiral presented it me with pleasant words, what time he kept in head & firmly embraced me on both cheeks – It being the custom in France to hug the tommy you decorate –

Its rather a nice bronze medal – I'll show it you when I come home which will be about 25th Aug: Mrs Wynne got one too – I enclose a bit of the ribbon.

[12 August 1915]

This ribbon is still attached to the letter.

She admitted to her father she was feeling 'rather a rag lately, back aches & things & get tired over nothing – it's a pest and I'm slacking & taking things easy in the hope it will go – It's such a bore feeling cheap ... here as it interferes with everything,' but told her father not to be anxious 'as it is pots better already'.

But she was not well. She was aware that one of her sisters was ill for the second time in a few weeks and this was compounded by the fact that Dorothie had forgotten her mother's birthday. She was still doing do night work, felt lazy and described her mind as blank. Dorothie was definitely ready to go home.

Dr Jellett was so concerned that he had persuaded Dorothie to see a physician in London. As he had lived in the same house for some time, he was aware of her period problems, her recurring pain 'in my underneath' and although would not have discussed her deep thoughts with him, he could tell that she was sometimes depressed. He had always been concerned about her eating habits and as she was not recovering from the back problem as quickly as he liked he decided to take action, no doubt with the support of the countess. Surprisingly, Dorothie put up no resistance, but she still tried to assure the countess there was little wrong.

Dont worry – I'm not dead – or likely to be for the next century – only Dr Jelly just wanted me to go to the bloke in London on my way down as being simpler than leaving it till later – So you mustn't think please, its because there's anything the matter, because there aint – Its just because I'm that amiable (ahem) you know I always do as requested.

[20 August 1915]

But there was something the matter and it must have been very serious. Dorothie was at Newnham for two months.

6

GOODBYE TO THE MARINS

When Dorothie decided to return it was obvious that her family were still concerned about her and she was yet again trying to reassure her mother who had, somewhat reluctantly, driven her down to London.

You were a darling to drive me down yourself & see me off thank you so very much – As to my 2 months of idling & being waited on – words fail me – to tell you how nobly you bore with me & spoiled me.

It has given me a new lease of life especially morally – & that it mostly due to you & home sympathy – I really am feeling ever so much more fit mentally – & after all it's one's brainpower & willpower that carry you – or let down your body as it did mine.

But home has overhauled it & it can go on for ever now – I shall be glad of work again.

I will write more tomorrow.

God bless you many many times.

[22 October 2015]

Her brother Peter had been instructed to call on her and try to persuade her not to return for a while. Dorothie told her mother that she was out when the wire had arrived about his proposed visit. Although she was sorry to miss him there is something in her tone that indicates that, just for once, she was trying to avoid him, because she believed he might win her over. She did not want to change her mind about going back. 'I am so sorry to miss him – Its real hard lines, & he might have chosen it more tactfully.' The morning after she dined with her uncle, he and her sister Mollie 'bundled me into my train', neither of them attempting to change her mind.

Unfortunately, she had just received some news about Mellins' brother Bill Harding. He was not dead but was going to be crippled for life. She had known Bill all her life and this news was very upsetting, just as she felt able to return. At least she heard that she was needed in Furnes.

I hope you understand about my not coming back again – I honestly feel it would be better for me to get on & do something just now when I happen to be wanted to arrange things ... Goodbye Mother dear & a big big prayer from Diddles – for you have such a terrible hard time in the war – I feel I should be more use to my family washing up plates then dodging Fritz in Flanders!

[23 October 1915]

Her return was full of incident, and she was nearly arrested on landing, omitting to get one document that she said had been 'invented' since she had last crossed the Channel. She excused herself by saying there was not time to get it at Folkstone, so she just caught the boat in spite of the officials who had wired ahead to Calais to warn them that a suspicious character was on board. On arrival, they refused to let her land. The result was as dramatic and enjoyable as most of Dorothie's escapades and her eventual arrival no doubt cheered her up immensely.

To our joy & amusement a clearance officer & two hairy sentries with bayonets came & arrested us in the cabin & said we weren't to land!! – But it all petered out by their receiving an answer from the Belgian GHQ 10 minutes later in answer to their enquiries saying not to be a fool & let me off. I went & saw the others yesterday, who Jelly hadn't told I was coming to surprise them & they were struck all of a heap when I strolled in.

Charles is frisky & a bit scabby – & delighted to see me.

Hélène & Zenobie nearly off their rockers with excitement – bless them.

I saw the general too yesterday who sent you his love, said to thank you again for a charming letter you had written him. It appears the Mission had quite made up their minds I had gone for good now, so I must go & cock a snook at them just to show there is no ill feeling.

Torrents of abuse on all sides for being le dernier des derniers of slackers & being away so long.

[26 October 1915]

Hély d'Oisel sent his regular invitation to visit him at Bethune and 'loffly lots of cigarettes' were waiting for her. She was pleased to be back and explained again to her mother why she needed to return.

> ... oh thank you more & more in all your dearness to me – I cant say all I feel – but your love & sympathy have helped me so much – I feel I just must have active work to do, or I couldn't keep up – on the other hand I feel we have deserted you, & left you all the hard & dreary work, with everyone gone – I wish I was more help.
>
> [27 October 1915]

Her return marked a change in the weather. 'Such mud! Such rain'. She looked out her bedroom window to a 'vista of fields and mud, mud, rain & mud, lorries splashing mud, pot holes on the road full of mud & 'Daniel' a mass of mud ... mud is a Flanders speciality.' But it did bring gorgeous rainbows in the dunes and created a scene which she likened to a 'fine H Majesties theatre effect – the dunes with the sun shining on them – the mist lifting – a huge double rainbow in the middle'. Dorothie could always see the beauty round her and even a shell bursting was described as a 'fine black splotch against the rainbow – most futuristic'.

Dorothie was relieved to find the Corps, so often chaotic and badly managed, had been well run in her absence – 'divers rifts seem done'. Matters were now being run on more businesslike and economical lines. They had a big meeting and the mood ¬s amicable, and she hoped that this would continue. Charles ⸗ntertaining as ever and his newest trick of sitting on the coal box amused Dorothie, chosen because 'it is near the stove & fuggy and makes nice patterns on my clothes'.

Dr Jellett had been busy in Dorothie's absence:

The work seems going very well & old Jelly is certainly running it far more thoroughly & competently than Bevan did – of course now its easier there are less people – but things badly wanted sorting out & as long as Bevan was boss one couldn't interfere – I am going to see the hospital to-day – The house here now boasts what Hélène calls a 'Oh Hell clock' – beats Marjies into fits – Rather clever of Jelly – It was in bits – part woodwork broken & works all 'anyow – He collected same & has got the thing working after much labour – & I gather 'Oh Hells' – hence Hélènes christening of it! – But the result is magnificent –

Also my bedroom now boasts of a fine oak panelled e–nor-mous washing stand with marble top complete!

It is true the front of one side is entirely missing due to an obus, but the rest is very 'rich' looking – & if one remembers not to put the 'pots, indiarubber – handles without, lunatics for use of' in front of the hole, ahem, it is all right.

[27 October 1915]

However, she was not relieved by the news of the war. At the Front nothing had been gained by either side, 'absolutely no change in my absence except very heavy losses & nothing to show for it'. The Germans had continued to shell the little towns along the Front and her beloved Marins had suffered heavy casualties. Dorothie continued to be close to danger and survived near misses, but as ever she played the danger down. One afternoon a shell had burst just behind her car damaging it slightly, but she was unhurt. 'Such is life – who cares.'

Everything seemed dismal, especially the weather, which was wet and cold. The wind was the sort that 'blows right through you – in at your boots and out by the ___'. News of Mellins' brother Bill was not hopeful and even her garden provided no pleasure: 'It is very sad & desolate only a few mingy nasturtiums to represent its past glories – it is depressing.' On 29 October she reported to her mother that Jelly was in a bad temper, which she also found depressing. She even considered that she might, too, be in a bad temper. Nevertheless, this was balanced by the pleasure expressed by Hélène when Dorothie returned. She had thought Dorothie would not come back until the spring because of the mud and was overjoyed when she returned so soon, and Hélène's son helped the household to counter the gloom. He was four and according to Dorothie 'an awful nut'. He lived at No 14 as Dorothie did not like him being in the bombarded part of town with his aunt. She had bought him a smart brown jersey and knickerbockers and a tin of bull's eyes from Selfridges, and he was obviously thrilled with his gifts.

Aware of her mother's continuing concern Dorothie provided an update on her health:

P.S. It is lasting well – & I am not doing too much – no night work – only one regular round to N— in the afternoon & sometimes gadgets in the morning – I am feeling much stronger everyday & not over tired – I promise you to go easy for some time yet.

PPS & then just as I get right I shall probably be bagged by Fritz – which would be a 'bit hard' wouldnt it?

[1 November 1915]

She was also eating well on and catching up with her friends. 'I have just had an e–normous lunch in the British Mission – All very affable & very pleasant & old Teck full of beans – Very good lunch too & I am as full as an egg.' Hély d'Oissel was also at the lunch and was going to arrange for her to visit her brothers at Bethune and with this to look forward to, it was a very happy day.

Yet again, there was depressing news of loss. This time it was about her beloved Admiral Ronarc'h, the commander of the Fusiliers Marins. Not death but nearly as awful – departure.

Alas – it is only too true – The Admiral is being given a sea command & the whole brigade broken up & sent back to the Navy as they can no longer spare the personelle.

I can't tell you how truly grieved & sad I am – It is impossible to work so long for such a magnificent set of men as they have been without becoming deeply attached to them – I do not mean to individuals as you know they have always been such good friends to me I shall miss them dreadfully – But also the Brigade in the 'abstract' – They are such a splendid lot & I love them all – They have been such a 'moral', & such a gallant crowd – & I feel like them as Rollo does for his Coldstreams – It is like a bit of oneself – & I feel just as sad as seeing them go as he was to see his Guards Brigade leave him – or still worse be disbanded.

[Date and first page missing]

Despite the religious doubts Dorothie had voiced earlier in the year she took comfort from attending Mass, and the activities of one or two of the faithful provided her with a great deal of entertainment.

I am just feeling as flat & backboneless as a kipper having been squashed so flat at mass just now – It was in a tiny chapel bursting with bulgy belges of both sexes and all smelly like bad margarine – no room to stand let alone sit or kneel – & if anyone can raise a prayer under these conditions they arent human.

So I gave it up half way & have come in to write to you instead – Anyway I feel less profane so doing & I expect you agree?

Anyway the margarine smell is slowly dying away which is always something – I can say a Deo Gratias for that with proper fervour, if I can't for anything else.

[1 November 1915]

And on another occasion:

At mass this morning my prayers were interfered with once more – This time it was an old lady kneeling next to me, who kept flopping down with a wump – saying one Ave about & then diving out of the church for about 30 seconds, & then coming back again – I think it must be that awful habit initiated by some infernal Pope, whereby the faithful are obliged to pay 58 visits to the church, & get even with the system by coming in & out one after another – I know it's a game the convent children always play in holy week – Anyway this old lady had it bad, & by the 42nd time she had come in out I started getting palpitations from the nervous strain.

It is very like Potter [a dog at Newnham Paddox] when he decides at 2 am he wants to go out in the garden & vomit, & walking round & round the room for hours till you get up, making pattering noises with his nails on the linoleum!

[2 or 3 November; D. isn't sure]

When she was not being interrupted, she was praying for the wounded and dead. Her special prayers were for her beloved Marins.

Yesterday there was heavy firing at N.— about 3.30 pm – Fritz shelled the Marin trenches with fury for ½ an hour, & Mennenwafer [*minenwerfer*] & trench motor 'torpilles' too, & a lot of rifle fire – But they didn't attack – so I don't quite know why they did it – The poor marins lost a good many men, about 30 or 40 & four officers – killed & wounded.

Fritz had been doing this every 2 or 3 days all October they say – Never attacks, but shells a small bit of trench each time very heavily, just as if they were preparing an attack.

It is not surprising that Dorothie's appetite was a concern to her mother. It seemed that she had a lack of interest in food and missed meals because she could not be bothered. On occasions, her reaction was to overeat until she was at the point of nausea. On 4 November Dorothie had just eaten 5 lbs of marron glacés. 'I can't describe to you the feeling of satisfaction – reflection & nausea that have taken possession of me as a result – I'd sell my soul for maron glacés any day & as Jelly & Charles don't like then I eat the lot which is so satisfactory.' Dr Jellett was continually concerned about Dorothie's appetite and watched over her, to her evident annoyance, as we have already seen.

> By the way please pay no attention to Jelly & my old appetite – he has it on the brain! – I never do eat much out here – Dont need to somehow – its only at NP [Newnham Paddox] one wants to eat for 10! – out here I need ½ the food & sleep I do at home always – What with you telling Jelly I'm to have Bengers [a restorative food for invalids] which I hate – & the Gen I'm not to have marons glacés which I love – death is losing its sting.
>
> [4 November 1915]

Dorothie's lack of appetite for long periods followed by gorging huge amounts of food, especially not nutritious, would be identified today as an eating disorder, often brought on by trauma and distress. There are also less dramatic causes. Excitement and lack of time can either kill the appetite or cause overeating. The former was true of Dorothie and in ordinary circumstances her body would have reverted to a natural balance. However, the continual stress of the war years, with constant heightened awareness and the irregularity of her daily life, exacerbated Dorothie's health problems.

Her mother had obviously enlisted the help and support of her companions and they tried their best to encourage her to eat properly but they were disadvantaged by Dorothie's strong, powerful personality and her charming dismissals of their concern.

Dorothie enjoyed the meals with those who she called 'one's own', the General, the Prince of Teck and her many officer friends. Away from the noise and reminders of war she relaxed, enjoyed the conversation, drank wine and ate a normal meal. Unfortunately, that was the exception. Most of the time she was forced into an irregular timetable, dashing around and constantly facing death and danger in the most terrible weather conditions, picking up wounded soldiers; the last thing on her mind was food. Even when there was lunch it was not what her mother would have described as substantial.

> Such a wet day to-day. Fritz inactive & besides shooting at Furnes which he can't miss with his eyes shut he hasn't been at all offensive – I was too energetic for words today and spent from 9.30 to 4 pm with lunch interval for 'oxo' under Daniel on my turning, scraping the mud off with a coal chisel – Jelly upside down the while in the engine girds – the result is magnificent & Daniel clean inside & out & he doesnt know himself.
>
> [9 November 1915]

For all of the time that Dorothie spent in Flanders, her appetite, or lack of it, exercised the minds of her friends whose gentle reminders would not annoy her, and the impatient and irascible Dr Jellett, whose would.

There was always news of death and one report really concerned Dorothie. During an attack on Furnes there were reports of death and injuries in which an English girl had been wounded and a Belgian woman killed. Elsie Knocker and Mairi Chisholm, two of the original members of the Corps, were now based in Pervyse and a local man had 'dashed up' to them and told them that the English girl was Dorothie. Distraught, they dashed down to check and were extremely relieved to find out this information was false. But the reports were accurate about the soldiers and other civilians.

> To-day & yesterday tragedies at Furnes – Yesterday they shelled the town & A soldier was killed not far from here – Today a lot of aeroplane bombs dropped in our district again – & hit slightly two English ladies (The Red X) newly arrived who have been feeding the poor Belgian refugee kiddies at a 'lean to' school some 500 yds from here.
>
> They aren't bad I believe – it happened while I was at it today – But a Belgian lady working with them at the same work was killed I am sorry to say.

Those pretty towns and villages that Dorothie had first seen in October 1914 were gradually being destroyed. On 5 November:

> I went to R__capelle to day the 1st time since my return – Ye Gods what a mess! – You know it was knocked to blazes while I was at home – there wasnt much then to wave yr arms about – but now it is pathetic – There is scarcely a bit of wall left to take cover behind now – & all the old 'postes' & the divers sheltered nooks 'Daniel' used to be bathed in, are flat!

Worse still, the inhabitants were suffering badly from the continued shelling and consequent destruction. Dorothie did all she could to alleviate their awful conditions.

I have been giving lots of the kiddies scarves & things round N__.

They are so bucked poor little souls – The next door to us is a family of Mama & her married daughter living together in a wee cottage – Population is nine kids under 14!! So you can see you must be thankful for only 2 stugs at N.P.! – The husband was killed at Furnes & they are terribly poor – so I do what I can for them.

Tell Bettie if there are any old children's warm clothes at home, jerseys etc. They would be so grateful for them.

[5 November 1915]

On 15 November Dorothie received a visit from Elsie Knocker and Mairi, which took her mind completely off the war.

They came in & sat on my bed bursting with excitement & Mrs M proceeded to apologise for all the divers unpleasant remarks she ever made to me & to swear she never meant them & wouldn't do so again.

Much surprised I marvelled exceedingly & then the reason – She is engaged to a Belgian 'Lieut Baron Harold de T'Serclaers de Rattendael' & it is now announced & she is in a devil of a flutter – It appears he is young & an Apollo & is of 'a most noble' family, & quite ready to become a Protestant to please me my dear – isn't it sweet of him? But I think it might make unpleasantness out here if he did – so I shall become a Catholic instead – & I want you to tell me how to do it etc.'!!!!

Can't you see me, missioning Mrs K ! –

I at once assured her she had far better leave everybody's concerned religion as it was for the moment & think it over a little more! – Anyhow she intends to get married some time before the spring & will probably live at La Panne.

It would not be in Dorothie's nature to gossip, but her comments on Elsie's news and apology reveal that Elsie's relationship with Dorothie had been less than friendly. Although she had never written anything disparaging in her letters about Elsie Knocker – in fact she had praised her commitment on occasions – she may have talked to her mother about her when on leave. The countess would have remembered that on her visit to the Front, Dorothie was rather rude about Elsie when she walked into the cellar and said, 'Here's Mother'. She would therefore understand Dorothie's sardonic comments.

It could be argued that Elsie appears to be exhibiting an element of snobbery, marrying into the aristocracy and hoping to acquire the veneer that was natural to Dorothie, who was not snobbish about her aristocratic background; she accepted it as normal. For centuries, some of the nobility adhered to the duty and service that had been instilled into them, and Dorothie's work in Flanders fulfilled this duty. Her Catholic upbringing had taught her respect for mankind and that everyone was equal under God, and she therefore treated everyone in the same manner as she would her equals. Added to this was her good nature, sense of fun and enjoyment of life and with all this came one extra skill – invaluable in times of stress and anger. Within minutes she could take the heat out of any argument, settle differences of opinion, and make peace in any awkward situation, and – vitally important – leave all the antagonists feeling as they had not been diminished. And although she was quick at thinking and taking action, she acted without panic.

Very few people could have truly disliked Dorothie. Her actions may have irritated certain people, for example, the doctor in a funk, Fitzgerald whom she annoyed when trying to bend the rules to visit her brother, and of course, Dr Jellett, but none of them would have disliked her because of her background. The exception was Elsie Knocker.

Elsie was in many ways similar to Dorothie. She was adventurous, courageous and had been eager to get involved in the war – 'There is work to be done'. Dorothie adored horses; Elsie adored motorcycles. She was an experienced rider and had taken risks in her life before the war and she used all these skills and characteristics in Flanders where her courage was rewarded with a medal. Her nursing skills were excellent and the soldiers she rescued adored her, calling her 'The Angel of the Trenches'. She stayed, with her friend Mairi, until the end of the war, and when on leave raised huge amounts of money to support the work. In these circumstances her middle-class background was not a disadvantage to her. However, it was probably her own personality that led to her dislike of Dorothie. Elsie was not well-connected – she was not the friend of monarchs, generals, aristocracy and officers – and it annoyed her to see Dorothie being able to get things done because of her background, situations where Elsie would have had no power or influence. Elsie was jealous of Dorothie, who unwittingly made it worse by usually responding with charm and respect. Therefore, in Elsie's eyes, her forthcoming marriage to Baron 'Lieut Baron Harold de T'Serclaers de Rattendael' was a triumph. She would be elevated to the same rank as Dorothie and she could not resist dashing to Furnes to tell her. Dorothie might have tartly remarked that it was rude of anyone from any rank to burst unannounced into her bedroom, but with good grace allowed Elsie to enjoy her happiness and diplomatically gave her best advice on Catholic conversion.

In the present circumstances there were very few women with whom Dorothie could become friends and with whom she could spend her leisure hours. The nurses lived at the hospital and were extremely busy and spare time for them was difficult. However, the arrival of Esther McNeil pleased Dorothie. Esther was the daughter of an MP who was known to the Denbighs and Dorothie promised to help her as much as she could. 'She is such a nice girl.' Esther had come out to run a clothing and distribution centre for refugees that also gave the children free food. She moved into a house only 300 yards away, sharing with Mrs Innes Taylor, whose nerves 'have been to pot' since a recent shelling attack. 'She is very jumpy as a result & I don't expect will get over it' – but Dorothie was pleased that McNeil was 'absolutely normal from that point of view'.

On 18 November, Dorothie and Dr Jellett were invited to supper with the Marin doctors to say goodbye. From experience she assumed there would be 'an awful orgy of at least 25 courses & divers drinks & many speeches'. Fortunately, in light of her dietary swings, it was not gargantuan.

I am glad to say it was not such an orgy as was expected! & I got off with only 4 different coloured drinks & a liquer that was so strong – God knows what – it nearly gave me an heart attack.

Then speeches at the end aimed at you & you feel you'd like to fall thro' the floor – you know the kind! – But they said many kind things about what we had done for them & how sad they were to leave – and they meant it too which was nice of them – Then they drank my health 'la brave – la dévousé at la charmante' & I had to try & tell them what fine chaps they were too etc. only I didn't do it half so well.

This morning a little revue in the dunes at which H D'Oissel said goodbye to the brigade Marins – A march past of Zouaves & Marins etc with their flag – & it made me very sad indeed to realise it was the last time they would 'defile' anywhere any more. I just love my marins & get sadder & sadder as it is time for them to leave – In a fortnight there will only be the one battalion & a few odd people left to represent the Brigade flag – It will be nice to have just a few 'poms poms rouges' about the place still.

She was going to miss her Marins. The Germans were also going to 'miss' them, and Dorothie was amazed at their up-to date information. 'It's extraordinary how the Bosch knows everything that is going on. Several days ago he shouted over to the Marins in their trench "I say when are you going away? We thought you had gone." This before the men themselves even knew they were being taken away!'

The Marins started to leave and were gradually replaced by a Zouave regiment. Dorothie was upset enough to write to her mother that she felt like shooting them all. She apologised for not writing properly for several days and explained that there was always someone 'bounding in' at No. 14, probably Marins, to say goodbye.

It is too sad – I just cant bear saying goodbye to them well – They have all been so wonderfully nice to us – & they are my own particular regiment – Even if the Admiral hadn't been promoted they would have been disbanded as they cant spare naval officers for infantry any more – You can make a good infantry officer in a few months – but the same amount of years to make an efficient naval officer.

The Admiral tore back for the afternoon here 2 days ago to say goodbye – He came without any warning & called at NO. 14 but I was at N__ – Luckily I got a message saying he was at his H.Q. & would I go at once – so I legged it with Daniel & got there just in time to see him for 5 minutes before he left again – He was so sad at going – & we were all very sorry too – He was such a nice mixture of capability (from military point of view) courage – & absolute simplicity minus all swank, that made all his officers & men adore him – as a result he got everything from his men, where many might have not nothing.

[23 November 1915]

The Admiral was also feeling very sad about going and possibly not seeing Dorothie again: 'The old boy said many kind things to before he went off – & then said to me run away quick as was so sorry to see me go – So I fled.'

On 28 November she had managed to visit Rollo and Peter at Bethune and she was delighted as she had not seen them for three months. After a lunch and afternoon together, she

1. The ten Feildings, 1902. Right to left: Rupert (Rollo), Hughie (or Neb), Mollie (or Moll), Dorothie (Dodo or Diddles), Agnes, Marjorie (Marjie), Henry (Peter), Clare (Squeaker), Elizabeth (Betty) and Victoria (Taffy).

2. Newnham Paddox, Monks Kirby, Warwickshire – the Denbigh home.

3. Dorothie's parents, Rudolph Feilding, 9th Earl of Denbigh and the Countess of Denbigh *née* The Hon. Cecilia Mary Clifford.

4. Mollie, Hughie and Dorothie rowing on the lake.

Above: 5. The Feilding children and friends performing a play. Dorothie is seated, end of row on right.

Left: 6. Cartoon drawn by Lord Baden Powell of Dorothie fishing on the Dove, Derbyshire. Baden Powell and the Feildings were close friends and often visited each other's houses.

TROUT
    FISHING
on the Dove   : 18. JUNE. 1908

Above is a sketch of Lady Dorothie Feilding fishing drawn By General Baden Powell

7. House guests at Swainsley Hall, Ashbourne, home of Sir Thomas Wardle, a close friend of the Feildings. The signatures are those of the guests in 1908.

Above left: 8. Dr Hector Munro, creator of the Flying Ambulance Corps.

Left: 9. Hughie in the naval uniform of lieutenant-commander.

Below left: 10. Lieutenant-General Sir Tom Bridges. He was involved in the first British battle of the war at Mons, and later commanded the 19th (Western) Division during the Battle of the Somme in 1916 and then in the Battle of Passchendaele the following year. He later became the nineteenth Governor of Southern Australia. Despite his own heroism he did not recognise Dorothie's and remained impervious to her charms.

Below: 11. Mairi Chisholm, Dorothie, and Helen Gleason – waiting for orders.

Above left: 12. Commander Henry Halahan, known as The Bloke, a close friend and confidant of Dorothie. He was in charge of the naval siege guns on the Flanders coast.

Above right: 13. Dorothie in uniform and ready for action.

14. A Darracq ambulance at Grande Place, Furnes. Dr Jellett is looking at the camera and Dorothie is in the driving seat.

15. The garden at No. 14 was a place of peace which Dorothie filled with daffodil bulbs from the countess, to which she added plants, flowers and shrubs. She was not averse to bribing a 'red-haired urchin' with toffee to climb over someone's wall and steal some lilac with no questions asked.

16. Dr Jellett and Dorothie enjoying afternoon tea and cake. Her early training in housekeeping skills is in evidence with the table set properly for afternoon tea: uncreased tablecloth, teapot, milk jug and white china teacups. Charles sleeps peacefully on the chair.

17. Dorothie and a Belgian policeman discussing the damage to an ambulance from a German shell.

18. Impressive-looking defences before shells and the weather take their toll.

19. A hollow created to hide an artillery observation post in the dunes.

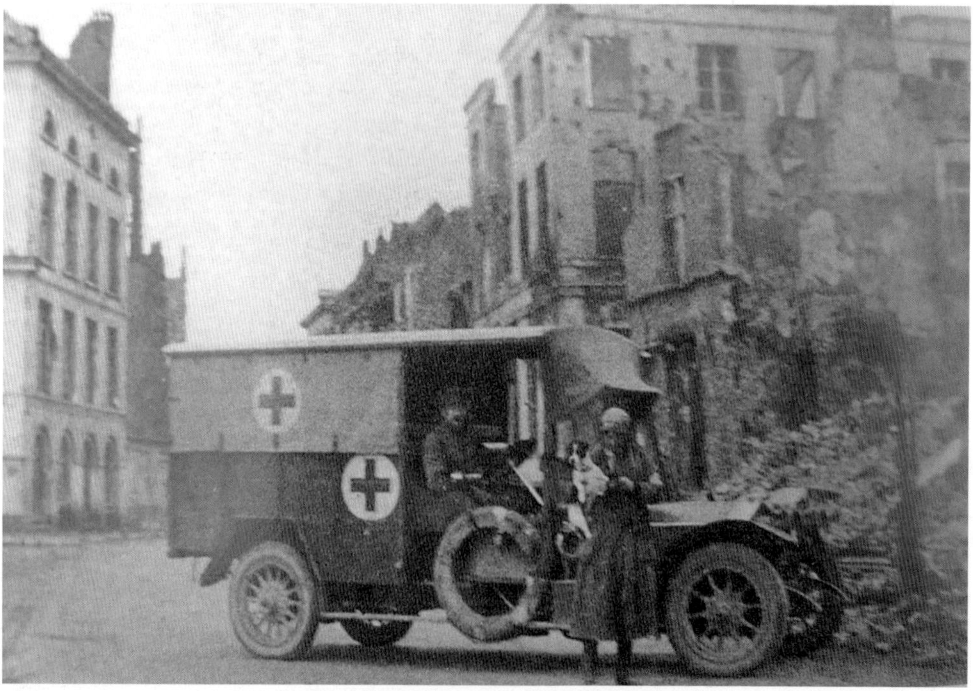

20. Dorothie, Charles, Jack Secker and 'Daniel' at Ypres, 1915. The ambulance may have been converted from a French Darracq motor car.

Above: 21. A day of rest for Dorothie and Charles; in the distance shelled buildings of Ramskapelle.

Right: 22. 'Recently decorated with the Order of Leopold: Lady Dorothie Feilding.' *Illustrated War News*, 1915. On her right is Dr Shaw and on her left John Secker. She is wearing a German shell fragment as a trophy.

TELEGRAMS & CABLES
SELFRIDGE, LONDON.

TELEPHONES ARE CONNECTED WITH EVERY DEPARTMENT
when ORDERING please call "GERRARD 1, ORDER DEPA[RT]"

TELEPHONE
GERRARD "ONE."

Bought of Selfridge & Co. Ltd
Oxford Street, London, W.

ACCOUNTS ARE DUE FOR PAYMENT ON OR BEFORE THE 10TH OF THE MONTH FOLLOWING PURCHASE, WITHOUT DISCOUNT.

Lady Dorothie Fielding,
Newnham
Lutterworth.

No. 47594

GHH	DATE	Nov. 1916	PRICE	PURCHASES	CREDITS
1331191	8	4 Casement	1/11½	7 10	
L O D	10	Postage		1 0	
557539	15	1 pr Breeches X		14 6	
L O D	16	Postage		1 0	
1141093	17	1 Pincher marten		3 6	
33281	22	1 Combination		8 11	
L O D	23	Postage		6	
1141093	25	1 cellar House of Pervyse		6 0	
1141093	29	1 Songs from Bks		5 0	
L O D	30	Postage		8	
				2.8.11	
12		To Oct. a/c		18.5	
2944				3.7.4	
Nov	27	Breeches			
Jan	7	* breeches returned –		14 6	
		By Cash		£2.12.10	
cheque enclosed				2.12.10	

Goods returned for Credit which reach us after the last day of the month, will be deducted from next month's account.

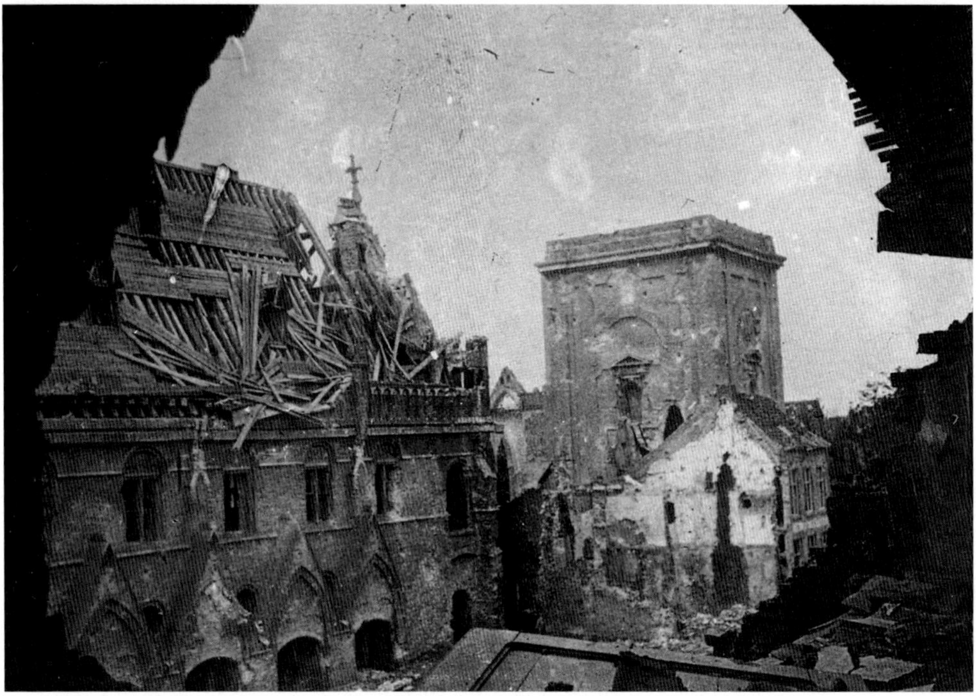

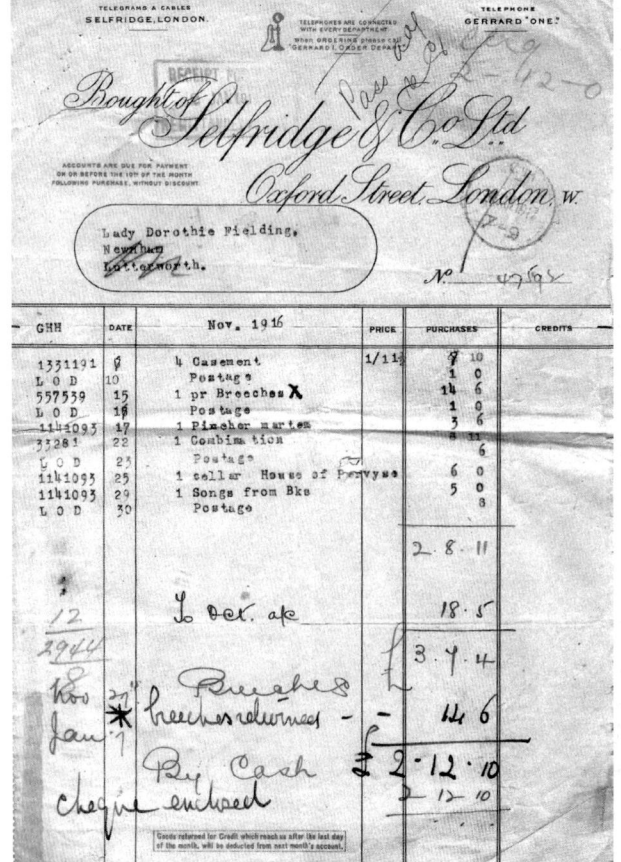

Above: 23. The Germans occupied Ramskapelle in October 1914 but were driven out by the Belgian 6th Line Regiment, supported by the 16th Battalion of French Hunters on Foot. The village was severely damaged leaving the station, the church and many houses in ruins.

Left: 24. The Denbighs had an account at Selfridges and Dorothie often sent for new clothing. The delivery address is 'cellar house of Pervyse'.

25. A short break for Dorothie with her friend and co-driver Lieutenant Robert de Broqueville on the way to Diksmuide.

26. Dorothie and Dr Jellett checking information with General Hély d'Oissel. Rear Admiral Pierre Ronarc'h looks on.

Left: 27. Mairi, Elsie and Helen smile as Dorothie and Dr Jellett check their cameras.

Below: 28. The centre of attention – Charles entertains officers of RAMC of 43 Division from Ypres.

29. The dug-out of the Belgian gunners in Ramskapelle.

30. Dorothie was inseparable from her Kodak camera. Taken near the lock complex at Nieuwpoort, on the back of this photograph she wrote, 'The ruins of a house in which 7 territorials were smashed by a 420 mm shell.'

31. Another woman who got closer to the front line than the military authorities thought necessary, Helen Johns Kirtland is pictured examining a spent mine near Ypres. She was an American photojournalist and war correspondent who competed with her male counterparts in her coverage of the war. She wrote an illustrated article, 'A Tribute to Women War Workers', explaining how women had helped the Allied cause. (Library of Congress)

Above: 32. President Wilson and Brand Whitlock, Minister and then Ambassador to Belgium, at Nieuwpoort, 1919. Wilson set out his dream for the future on that trip: 'Belgium's cause has linked the governments of the civilized world together... They have put the whole power of organized manhood behind this conception of justice which is common to mankind. That is the significance of the League of Nations.' (Library of Congress)

Right: 33. Dorothie and her eldest daughter, Ruth.

DOROTHIE MOORE
2nd DAUGHTER OF RUDOLPH
NINTH EARL OF DENBIGH
WIFE OF CHARLES MOORE
OF MOORESFORT TIPPERARY
BORN OCTOBER 6th 1889
DIED OCTOBER 24th 1935
SERVED IN THE GREAT WAR
1914 - 17 IN FLANDERS.
IN THE AMBULANCE CORPS.
BRITISH MILITARY MEDAL
CROIX DE GUERRE.
ORDER OF LEOPOLD OF BELGIUM
1914 STAR

34. Dorothie's grave in the Catholic Burial Ground, Newnham Paddox.

called in on her return to dine with General Hély d'Oissel and the next day went to stay with the Broquevilles for two days. She called it a depraved holiday, but the complete change from the noise and stress was better than any medicine. She went riding with Pierre de Broqueville, another of the General's sons.

The sense of tranquillity was punctured by tragic news. Bill Harding, brother of Dorothie's beloved sister-in-in law Mellins, had died.

> I am so terribly sorry about poor Bill & especially for little Mellins – These last weeks must have been awful for her – For Bill, he is spared the horror & the terror of being crippled – one seriously cannot wish that for anyone one cares for – It is the worst of all & a living death.
>
> Bill was always so tremendously alive & young & happy – I cannot very well realise it all. I went out to Mass & HC for him & Mellins today.
>
> [4 December 1915]

Concentrating on mundane requirements gave Dorothie a little relief from thoughts of Bill. She was searching for a kitchen clock and as the buildings were so badly damaged from the constant shelling, she was went looking in all the cellars:

> Here – all the shops or a great many go on selling their goods in the cellar – Even the jeweller of the town told me to-day he still has his things here – although his house with the exception of the basement has been properly smashed up by a shell a few weeks ago –

As all the inhabitants left I ca'nt quite see who his clients for tiaras are! But he assured me he still did quite a good trade.

[6 December 1915]

The departure of the Fusiliers Marins made Dorothie feel low and also brought change that was not at all to Dorothie's liking. She was very busy, but not rescuing wounded soldiers, which she would have preferred. Instead, she was involved with a lot of tiresome paperwork:

Have been interviewing all sorts of lousy officials all the week – on account of our taking over new work for the troops succeeding the marins – It isn't at all the same now – Then we were attached solely for their brigade of 6,000 & did entirely & solely for them & it was like a large family – Now our cars are attached to the Army Corps & just do a small part of the general work – The cars do as much – but it's not so individual or so pleasant – These officials too are all such fuss pots so different to the marins & always making silly complicated difficulties.

In fact we regret our marins more each day from every point of view & are all 'on the grievance' in consequence.

[10 December 1915]

Dorothie may have found the official fusspots irritating and Elsie Knocker trying, but she was very fond of Mairi Chisholm. She enjoyed the occasional 'jaw' with her, but disapproved of Mairi's adoption of nine refugee cats, which crawled over her chair and gave Dorothie a fright. Mairi was only nineteen years old and was very tough, but with Elsie's forthcoming marriage Mairi needed to think about her future. She and Dorothie were therefore delighted that Mairi's father, instead of suggesting that she go back home, told her he was coming up to help her. Dorothie would certainly have approved as she put such great value on her own family and their support.

Not all men had been so supportive. General Tom Bridges had been Head of the British Mission since the start of the war. He had always disapproved of women at the Front and was one of the few men who had never been swayed by Dorothie's charm. Despite her aristocratic background, her family's friendship with monarchs, her courage and bravery that had been so publicly rewarded, General Bridges' views remained unchanged. However, Dorothie always acknowledged people's good points and was never one to bear grudges.

Bridges & I haven't had a scrap for months & months, over the 'femme au front' question – That is all we ever fell out over – I always agreed with him entirely, but firmly declined to be moved! & all his divers tactics to move me were foiled!

Personally he has always been very nice to me – & he is a jolly good soldier & bound to do well.

[12 December 1915]

Amidst all these comings and goings, the second Christmas of Dorothie's life in Flanders was approaching and she was not due to take any leave. She sent a letter which must have touched her mother's heart.

I must write you for Xmas, though I cant believe it is upon us again – or so near either – But I want to wish you with all my heart that it wont be too sad & too anxious a one for you.

You have been such a wonderful person to all your various sons & daughters – You cant think how grateful we are for all your love & help through life – The Almighty really was splendid the way he chose our parents – without so much as one of us on the spot to arrange it either! Poor mother – the war has brought you many anxious hours I fear – but please God it will be over some day, & it is a little better now the 2 boys have safe billets & you needn't be so terrified for them.

Soo goodnight Mother dear, & God bless you more times than I can say for all your love & sympathy – Indeed I'm grateful & you know it dont you?

Yr so loving
Diddles

You mustn't worry about me you know – I haven't been obused, not close, for weeks & weeks & weeks & weeks. Really & truly s'help me, as Neb says.

[18 December 1915]

Just before Christmas the Germans attacked.

Fritz has woken up these last 2 days – To-day he threw 900 obus round poor old N__ but no one seemed to mind in the least & yesterday he had quite a little hate & chewed up the roads a lot – one place getting over the debris to-day, the poor old ambulance 'Daniel' had to do the prettiest bit of alpine climbing he's met yet in Flanders – Got stuck too on Mont Blanc & had to get gunners to push us off.

One battery of french '75 had got real hell nearby – Every gun shelter knocked to Jerico, & a mess of twisted girders, sandbags, & debris round & on each gun – & yet not one damaged to matter & no-one hit – It is one of the best escapes I've seen for a long time – & how the guns weren't put out of action permanently defeats me.

The gunners were very bucked to-day, told us proudly they had dragged the guns out from the décombes safely at night & had put them up in a new position nearby. & were just going to have a pip at Fritz to say 'Yaa Boo' & show they were none the worse! – They were perfectly delighted with themselves!

Yesterday at 4 a.m. the germans started a gas attack – on all the gens troops to the right of the Belgians & the English lines down to opposite Ypres – But everyone was expecting it & they opened a diabolical artillery fire, so that the Germans were never able ever to leave their trenches.

[20 December 1915]

And, as usual, she finished with the most matter-of-fact information; that she was dining with the General that night.

The countess was glad of these small diversion in her daughter's life but knew that Dorothie was still troubled by the deaths of her close friends. In one of her letters to her daughter the countess discussed life after death but, despite her mother's attempts to comfort her, Dorothie still could not reconcile herself to the concept of the afterlife.

You said in one letter, that with the dead one is much nearer to them than before, & that one looks forward to meeting them again – But mother, try as I will, I just can't make myself believe really & truly in my heart & hearts that we shall any of us ever see them again – I think there is just an endless blank that begins after death & that all things finish there.

I try to believe that there's a future, but I ca'nt any more – I suppose its seeing so many lives go out in their youth & strength, like the wind blowing out a light – People were, & they are not – & that is all.

While alive one must do ones best to help everyone, & that is best done by doing right – but why we should expect or need anything after I really can't see?

[21 December 1915]

Dorothie was struggling to deal with her thoughts when alone. She made great efforts to cope with her distress and went to the chapel as often as she could to pray. Even company offered little comfort and, deeply despondent, she declined the Broquevilles' invitation to spend Christmas with them. 'They came to carry me off on Xmas day but I put it off, because I didn't want to go anywhere – I should only have felt homesick, while up here one just goes on as usual & its all right.'

Instead, she went to Mass. 'Xmas eve I went to my Marins midnight mass which was very beautiful & impressive – just a little ready made altar, & a big crucifix all smashed by shelling, & nothing but the Marins, who sang hymns in Breton & all of them came.'

Perhaps this helped to lighten her mood as Christmas was better than she hoped.

Here I had quite a nice Xmas – Lunch at 12-30 in a hurry – a round to N__t with the car, where Fritz amused himself with obus, but total casualty one dent in a soldiers tin hat! – at any rate the only one in our vicinity – Then a dinner with the English sailors which was very nice – The 'Mish' had asked me, but I had already promised the sailors a long time ago – We had an absurd evening with a great battle with toy howitzers & dried peas as ammunition.

Charles was a great nuisance at the most critical moments of the battle, as he was feeling awful firstly & would dash in, devour the ammunition & try to slay the howitzers!

[26 December 1915]

Even at such a time, care had been taken with the décor: 'We even had pale pink candle shades – tho' it's true the candles were stuck on to phids of obus & the shades cut out of pink blotting paper by Ginger! Still it was very fine.'

Lady Denbigh had been planning a trip to Egypt to visit her husband and Dorothie was delighted that her parents would have some time together, but the trip was called off when Lady Denbigh was denied a permit to travel. Although Dorothie was sorry, it gave her a great opportunity. On 28 December, Dorothie decided to stay with the Broquevilles for a few days after all and whilst there wrote to her mother with undisguised glee.

I have a beautiful & lovely plot I have hatched, to make up for your not having gone to see Da.

It is that you & Squeaker come & see me!! Pa Broqueville & I have arranged it all & it is as follows – I am down here for a night.

1) You come & stay here (not far from Dunkirk) with Broqueville for a week – He is a week here & a week at

Havre attending so you have only to choose any of the times he would be here – He says he would be delighted to put you up any time after Jan 1st! You select – He suggested this scheme himself – You being Squeaker too of course – that is most important, & I promise you I won't take her to the lines or get either of you blown up.

2) Passes I will arrange for you – You wire me 'Delighted – could manage any day after__! – I then arrange with Broqueville the earliest date that fits with him – I sent you a letter from him authorising you to come which will secure you passports etc quite easily in London.

3) You go to Boulogne or Calais from when his car (me in it) brings you here. I will arrange to come & stay here then too of course & will give myself a few days holiday.

4) Then we will collect you a temporary pass & you & Squeaks will come & stay a night at Furnes at 14 – be introduced to Hélène & Charles – the General & all the rest.

5) Then you return here – get into a car when you like & return to Boulogne & voilà.

Total expense 3rd class ticket to Boulogne 25/- & I will stand Squeaks hers.

So Ma dear send me a wire please if you intend coming soon as it will take me a week to get the necessary passes over to you, & you a couple of days in London to get passports etc. visa'd.

Won't that be nice now? – So mind you do it – I should love to do you the honours of No 14 & so would Hélène & I would love to give little Squeaks a little jaunt to make up for Egypt falling thro'.

Now don't put it off like Da, or you will find NP a hospital & you tied down later on.

Furnes hasn't had a bomb or shell on it for 6 weeks & No. 14 being outside the town proper is as safe as Tooting now or I wouldn't write you. Also its a palace now & very comfy & a beautiful spare bedroom & Squeaks must get into mine & get up a proper fug together – So do please – please come – I shan't be back in England for months & months yet after my autumn leave – & it would do you good too.

[29 December 1915]

These plans came to fruition. To add to Dorothie's delight, her sister Claire (Squeaker) was accompanying the countess. Dorothie was ecstatic and threw herself in to the planning with energy and enthusiasm. Her next letters contained more lists and instructions, warned of possible delays, problems, suggestions of alternatives, people who they were going to meet and even advice on dress code. 'I forgot to tell you bring very few clothes, as all your kit has to go in the car – No evening kit or tea gown wanted at the Broquevilles as they don't change there for evenings – Just coats & sheets & a good warm motor coat.'

And Dorothie's plans included visits to various sites.

I will smuggle you up here for a few days & knock off work, as you wont be allowed in the lines now, its much stricter – But I can take you up to the English hospital – show you the beauties of Furnes, & get the General etc to come & see you here.

In fact if you or Squeaker feel it isnt warlike or exciting enough & disappoints you, I will sprinkle a few barbed wire entanglements round the bedroom, remove the mattress & the soap – break a window or two etc – In fact anything to please you.

One who would not be so pleased was Charles the dog, who was to be removed from the spare bed assigned to the countess during her stay. Dorothie's excitement is palpable and her spirits high.

7

A NEW FRIEND, SHELLS, FLEAS AND A FIELD OF POPPIES

Lady Denbigh and Squeaker returned to England after their week's visit, with items such as an 'obus' and coffee pots in their luggage to enrich the contents of Squeaker's Museum. Dorothie commented that she would be 'set up in copper goods for life', and despite Dorothie's plan to take her family to dangerous places they had a quiet and peaceful time. They were fortunate. Had their holiday taken place a few days later they would have faced the hazards of being near the Front and experienced what Dorothie faced almost every day.

Dorothie admitted feeling depressed after they had gone but the war soon took her mind off their absence. Just after they left, the Germans launched an attack in the area near Nieuwpoort.

Things have been humming a bit here since you left – The Boche took it into his head to attack <u>both</u> the General's sectors yesterday – He was repulsed, but got 30,000 obus off his chest, & cost us a good many casualties – They shelled poor N__ very badly indeed – one tower very broken & the other knocked clean down by 12 inches – There were about 150 casualties up this end, but the Boche did not get far – & had to give it up.

[23 January 1916]

Dorothie and Jellett had not been able to help on that day as they needed to repair Daniel's worn parts. They had just removed the five wheels and steering column when the firing started, and they could do nothing as it took until the evening to put him together again. On 25 January, they were able to take the wounded to a French base hospital she named 'IV'. The next day the French and Belgians launched 'a little hate to make up for one of Fritz's' and Dorothie recorded about 180 casualties. The English newspaper had suggested the Germans were making another bid for Calais but Dorothie, at 'the pulse of things', knew better and dismissed it as 'rot'.

Many refinements were missing from life at the Front, but personal cleanliness was very important to Dorothie. There was sufficient water and soap available for daily ablutions to take place, but the luxury of having her hair washed by a professional hairdresser was a real treat. She went to Dunkirk and sent Jellett to do the chores whilst she went to the hairdresser. 'I said to the fat lady who shampoos me, "My hair is very dirty isn't it?" She answered cheerfully, "Mais suit Mademoiselle et ça sent le poisson". Tell Squeaker that accounts for that curious smell of bloaters she complained about in "our" bed at 14.'

Another treat was the gift of a black swan. This caused Hélène two problems. First, she had never seen a black swan and was puzzled by what sort of beast it was and second, it would not fit into the oven. It was a strange item to find on the menu as black swans originate from Perth, Western Australia, and how this one arrived in this little corner of Flanders must have intrigued the inhabitants of No. 14. Dorothie was pragmatic about it. She obviously told Hélène to get it cooked, perhaps by cutting it in half, as there was no chance of Dorothie wasting food, even if her appetite was often lacking. 'If we die of indigestion you will know why – Charles will like it.' The swan was not wasted. It provided supper for several nights and had finally reached 'the soup stage & we are getting decidedly weary of him. Cooking swan too has a most curiously penetrating smell – & everything one touches from British warms to pyjamas has a pungent swan odour attached – I confess I'm rather tired of it.'

The smells of fish and taste of swan were minor distractions from the continual shelling. On 28 January, she reminded her mother of one or two buildings she had seen on her visit. 'There is only a fragment of Shoppee's tower left after that last shelling at __, & the 2nd one you saw from that mound is absolutely down – only a mound of bricks & I am sorry to say a French officer observer was killed in it.'

Other distractions were the occasional but welcome entertainments:

We had a concert for the blessés at Hoogstraat yesterday, given by different soldiers – It was quite good & of course the success of the evening as far as the blessés were concerned, was a vulgar man who sang about quite unmentionable subjects in quite unmentionable terms, in a piercing & very distinct voice!.

We took McNeil & the Saunders girl up with us.

[30 January 1915]

What Dorothie lacked was a female companion to live at No. 14. To stop gossip about her sharing only with a man, she had taken in Hélène the refugee girl, who was useful as a housekeeper, and another young girl called Zonobie. Dorothie described her as 'our tweenie', the title given to maids who did not have one specific job. Dorothie was very fond of them both and particularly liked Hélène's sense of fun and cheerful personality, which was a welcome foil to Dr Jellett's bad temper and constant nagging. But she needed a companion and as it was neither possible nor politic for a man to move in, Dorothie looked for the opportunity to offer a place to a woman.

Dorothie was not lacking in friends around her in Flanders, but because of the abnormal circumstances of war and her own specific role there were few women with whom to form friendships, as almost all her daily life involved dealing with men. And several of them were close friends that she already knew from her life before the war. They were from families who had been friends of the Denbighs and knew Dorothie well. She had been to school with the daughters of Broqueville and Hély d'Oissell and had frequently stayed at their homes in France and Belgium; Broqueville thought of her as his third daughter. She had not previously met Admiral Ronarc'h but it did not take long for him became one of her favourite people and for him to admire and respect Dorothie.

Other friends shared her social milieu; four officers who were in the Royal Navy Guns in Flanders, their company based in Nieuwpoort. Their commander was Henry Crosby Halahan, whom Dorothie always called 'the Bloke'. Halahan was a friend of the Denbighs and a close companion of her brother Rollo, and he and three of his lieutenants were constantly in Dorothie's company. They, too, had their nicknames. 'Ginger' was Desmond Tufnell, 'Deb' Arthur Casswell, Denys Shoppee had an odd enough name just to be 'Shoppee', and 'Burbidge' Arthur Brewill. Burbidge was in charge of a gun that Dorothie called 'Mother'. These officers were part of Dorothie's life until she finally left Flanders in June 1917. These men admired and respected Dorothie and may have loved her but there was no question of any romantic feelings. Buried deeply still was Dorothie's memories of Tom and his death, from which she still had not recovered. These friends were her pals, she treated them as she had treated her brothers and their friends before the war.

Nevertheless, Dorothie made attempts to get a woman to join them in No. 14. Esther McNeil was a possibility, she had to wait for the return of the Saunders girl who should have been coming back to live with Mrs Taylor, but after her experience she felt too nervous to return. This held up Esther's plans as Mrs Taylor could not be left alone, but she did agree that any friend of Dorothie was acceptable. Marjie had interviewed a woman called Molly Schreiber but Dorothie did not think she would be suitable. She was German and aged 30, which Dorothie considered too old, both Dorothie and Esther would have preferred a girl of Esther's age. Also, 'I fear she is rather "superior" & inclined to look down her nose.

I s'pose she would do it we can't find anyone else.' Marjie had also been asked to see another girl but had dismissed her as unsuitable. Dorothie expressed her annoyance to her mother and asked her to intercede.

There is this Speight girl Jelly writes you about – She sounds nice & is quite willing to come if you approve. I wrote Margie to … see her, & tell me how the girl struck her.

She really is a little fool – I told her to see the girl without committing herself to anything – It is absurd to turn the girl down without even seeing her – Age 25 – So will you please do something or if possible see the Speight girl yourself instead of Margie & tell me what you think of her before fixing anything up definitely with Molly Schreiber?

I will leave the decision to you as to whether the girl is nice or not. Marjie is so unbalanced at times!

I too don't want her if she isn't nice, but you can tell that in a minute – They are a good family & not dentists daughters as Margie seems to think!!

So please be a dear & get into touch with Margie about the Speight girl and if possible see her yourself as well as Margie – I should be very grateful if you would as soon as possible as things change so & letters take such ages.

[12 February 1916]

There is a gap in the letters from January until 1 May. Dorothie had been home on leave but approximately two months' letters are missing.

By 1 May, the issue had not been resolved. She wrote to her mother – in haste as usual:

Mother dear – I've written to Da about the Esther McNeil question – only dont say anything to her people yet – Should Mrs Taylor resent her coming to stay for dinner & heckling with me here as Esther things she probably will, she says she could probably get leave to just sleep here – Would that do? – or should one have someone more en évidence? Please let me have an answer to this as soon as you get it as she is expecting to hear from the other girl on leave any day about it.

We haven't asked Mrs Taylor yet, that's why I don't want it to get about until I have.

[1 May 1916]

Although Dr Jellett had suggested Winkie Speight as a possible candidate, Dorothie was concerned that he would think the Denbighs were not satisfied with him. Dorothie thought he was fussy, bad tempered, and uncouth, but she also knew that he was a good, caring man and had her best interests at heart. This was typical of Dorothie; she had the ability to assess people's characters, see the good in them, allow for their faults, and show gratitude to those who had helped her. It was also important to acknowledge her gratitude. She asked her mother to write to Dr Jellett and thank him for all his care and support and assure him that she would still value him in the future.

Whilst the issue of Winkie was taking up some of Dorothie's time, the war was also keeping her busy.

Day before yesterday an awful heavy bombardment down Dixmuide way from 4 a.m. till 6am. Shook even No. 14 – & I got up & expected Fritz into breakfast – Such a noise it was. We went down there after to see what was going on & took some blessés. Fritz had shelled very badly indeed – & took a trench – The Balgy Belge however pulled up his pants & to everyone's surprise counterattacked & took it back & made some Hun men & an officer prisoners. There were of course rather heavy casualties as a result of all the shelling.

Our cars carried 150 blessés last month – just been doing returns – Not bad for 6 people – We had an inspection yesterday by a new boss who complimented the unit on their efficient work & said he had no improvements to suggest as they weren't possible – They have done very well all the winter our little lot & are very bucked.

I was stuck for ¼ of an hour on the road while he shelled a bit of it ahead to blazes – Made nasty holes too – as if the road wasn't bad enough already – Eventually he was kind enough to let us by.

[3 May 1916]

The countess was not receiving the usual entertaining and lengthy letters from Dorothie and with this sort of news she could see Dorothie was very busy. But it was not the bombardment, the blessés or the shelling that prevented her from writing; it was something much more prosaic. 'Reason was I had lost my bee-loved pen. It has now turned up having secreted itself in a pair of 'pants – young thermals – wool throughout – Harrods Bargains Floor 3/11½'. Luckily, pants and pen intact so I can write again to the sainted Commandant with an easy mind.'

Dorothie was feeling happy because she was expecting a visit from her brother Hugh, who was on leave from the navy and took the opportunity to visit the front. He had once complained that he was 'stuck out' and his sister was right at the Front. He was taking the opportunity to see for himself what Dorothie was doing. She was also pleased by the arrival of a new ambulance. 'A Buick with an A1 body comprising every sort of folding – collapsible – not upsettable – labour saving – light weight – & squash your thumbs device. It blew in today being the gift of the "Wire Rope Makers Company" God bless them.' She was also delighted to hear that there was to be an exchange of British prisoners, one of whom was Margie's husband Dudley.

She was invited to lunch with Admiral Ronarc'h who had moved into a chateau belonging to the French Admiralty. The change for him amused her.

> ... a perfect joke & I laughed till I was quite ill! – One is accustomed to seeing him leading very much the simple life – whereas there he has a young Versailles – a chateau belonging to the French admiralty – all to himself – There are some 15 ante rooms & salons in pale green & gold etc & canopies that look as if they would crumple if you sat on them – It is so utterly unlike his old surroundings of dug-outs & wretched homes that everyone has a fou sourire whenever they see it – & he walks about with his hands in his pockets gazing at it in a lost kind of way.
>
> [8 May 1916]

She was even more delighted by his garden. 'He has a lovely huge garden with lots of flowers which has been placed at my disposal! I looted a large bunch of lillies of the valley & lilac to begin with.'

As always, there was some news that was not so welcome. Peter, her youngest brother, had transferred to the Coldstream Guards and would be moved to the Front. 'It means all that anxiety again – but I admire the boy for it & quite understand his point of view – He's a good lad to do it. But we were so glad to have them both out of it – That is life.'

Hugh's visit was a great success. He arrived on 14 May and spent the first day with Halahan as he was responsible for organising passes. Dorothie joined them for supper, and they spent the next few days together.

Had great fun with Hughie here – He will tell you about it – It was like a glorified Bank Holiday – we have been over everything & under everything & to see everybody – The only thing he hasn't seen is the war! – Fritz treated him with the same 'orrible respect he showed father & had been behaving like a stuck pig & refusing to fire anything at anybody to Hughies disappointment & our disgust! – as now he will never think we ever get hustled!

Burbidge came back from leave last night & supped here with the Bloke – The sailors have been perfect saints to Hughie doing him proud & getting him out here – Yesterday was just like a bank holiday picnic & the Bloke took Neb & I exploring & we had a most amusing day.

[17 May 1916]

When Hugh left Dorothie, he went right up to the Front where she was not allowed to go and she wondered how he had got on. 'I hope Fritz hustled him a bit to make up for the miserable politeness he showed him up this way!' Halahan had also organised a car to take Hugh down to see Rollo.

Hugh's visit had been peaceful but ironically, as soon as he left the air raids started.

> Great aeroplane raid in these parts last night – None in my little town – but in the one where Gladys & Margie were – Some 40 to 60 blessés.
>
> Bad business. We brought down one machine – The machines kept coming & going over us all the evening & much firing & searchlights all over the sky – I went to bed about 11 – but Hélène got up at 1 a.m. when they came again & retired to a dug out a few doors away with Charles under her arm & stayed till 3 a.m.! As she omitted to wake either Dr Jelly or me, I can only conclude she puts her values as above – which amused me muchly.
>
> [20 May 1916]

This was followed by another one at the Hôpital IV, a French military hospital in Zuydcoote (near Dunkirk) where Marjie and Dudley's sister Gladys had worked.

> They broke all the windows in Admiral Ronarch's new smart château – a bomb burst in the garden while he was at lunch & 1) broke the window 2) broke his rest in the garden & 3) killed the sailors mascots consisting of a magpie & a cat!
>
> Poor old Admiral – I think if one put him in an island in the Pacific bombs would diskiver him somehow – He is a sort of magnet for Fritz!

We brought down three german machines though – The English accounted for 2 & the allies one – so on the whole I consider we are up on the air raid.

There isnt much glass left in shop windows there now I hear.

[22 May 1916]

Every day there were incidents affecting the few inhabitants who chose to stay, adding to the gradual destruction of Furnes. She told her father that there had been a lot of firing on the road into Furnes where he had been with her on his visit, shelled heavily on 23, 24 and 25 May. 'One poor devil buried 7 metres deep under the debris of a cottage – of course killed. Some other men blesséd there too while we were in the tow & we took them along.' The anti-aircraft team redressed the balance by bringing five German planes down, which pleased the Belgians very much.

As in all wars, there were mistakes. On 29 May she was waiting in the gardens when an aeroplane flew overhead.

The town cloche rang saying everyone to his cellar – & all the anti-aircraft shot like mad with such vim it began to rain bits of shrapnel down on our heads in the garden here at 14 & drove us indoors – Then when it was all over – the plane came down & landed in a field close by & turned out to be an ally after all! – I wonder what the pilot had to say about it.

[29 May 1916]

Her mother's letter had given her the usual mix of good and bad news. Dudley's name had been put on list for exchange of German prisoners, which was 'perfectly splendid', but his father was not well, nor were members of the Feilding family: 'Just everyone seems to be getting ill these days.' Much worse was to follow. During the first days of June the Feildings received the most devastating news. Their beloved Hugh had been killed in the Battle of Jutland.

Of the five children actively engaged in the Great War, Hugh's involvement had caused the least concern and he had never faced such dangerous situations as Dorothie and Rollo. The Royal Navy had taken little part in fighting and the Battle of Jutland was the largest naval battle and the only full-scale clash of battleships in the war. It lasted for two days, and it was on 31 May that Hugh's ship, HMS *Defence*, the flagship of Rear-Admiral Sir Robert Arbuthnot, was leading the First Cruiser Squadron. Assisted by HMS *Warrior* they closed in on a crippled German light cruiser, the *Weisbaden*, but in doing so sailed right into the gun sights of a battlecruiser, SMS *Derfflinger* and four dreadnoughts. HMS *Defence* was battered

The end of SMS *Derrflinger*, the battlecruiser that destroyed HMS *Defence*, scuttled at Scapa Flow on 21 June 1919.

by heavy-calibre gunfire from the German battleships, which detonated her magazines in a huge explosion. She sank and all her crew, 903 officers and men, were lost. A tiny crumb of comfort for the families of those who died was that after such a massive explosion their deaths would have been instant.

On 3 June the countess wrote to Dorothie and it is clear that her deep faith was giving her support.

Darling –

God has taken back my beloved Hughie & a big gap is made in the family. He was so much to us all. But how much we have to thank for in having had him. Down to that very last leave of his when most of us saw him & he got the trip he so much wanted to make. Wanted most, next to his 'chance' & that too God gave him.

There is little to grieve for, when one thinks of all he was. Most one cries out thank God for the years we have had of him, with never a regret or anything but joy in them.

But all the same Diddles he has gone & we are here without him – the first sorrow we can trace to him! So we mustn't sorrow for he would not have liked us to...

Oh I am so glad he saw you & Rollo. He wrote me when he went back last autumn, 'I was so glad to have Diddles there. It is difficult to compare the seven delightful sisters you have given me but of them all I think she is the one who is most to me, & whom I love most & admire – God bless & comfort you darling ...

Yr loving Mother

Hugh had always adored Dorothie, he appreciated the danger she faced every day and was another member of the family who was concerned for her safety. On 6 May 1915, he wrote to Mrs Annan, the cook at Newnham Paddox.

Letters have just arrived from my wonderful sister in Belgium, poor girl, she has had a hard time lately with a lot of wounded & such dreadful wounds. It is hard for us up here to realise that all this is going on so close by.

I do hope she will be spared to us, but she runs so many risks in her unselfish work to attend the wounded; & it is miraculous that she had escaped so far.

It was ironic that Hugh had so badly wanted to be in at the heart of the action and that the navy spent most of the war on the periphery. It was Dorothie who faced terrible danger every day of her life, but when he came to visit her at the Front the Germans were very quiet; there were no shells exploding, no wounded soldiers to be rescued, and, as Dorothie said, it was just like a Bank Holiday. He would have seen the devastation and talked to the soldiers, but what it was like when the action started was all second-hand. The Germans waited until he left before recommencing shelling. When he finally got his wish to be at 'the heart of things', he was killed on the first day of battle. Dorothie went home for a month to be with her family and mourn Hugh.

She returned on 8 July and on the train wrote to her mother.

It was very nice of you & I loved seeing you – It was nice too seeing Hughies pals, Hall & dear old Freddy – his friends are like a tiny bit of him somehow – It hurts in a way, but one is so glad to see them all the same.

You mustn't worry about me darling – I will be as good as gold & not do silly things – Also I will come home oftener for little bits like this last time – You like that best don't you?

Going back this time to Flanders had none of the joy, expectations and the breathless excitement that filled her letters in 1914. The war was still going on but neither side was gaining anything significant. And there was the continual deaths and the wounded soldiers to collect from the trenches. There was small something to look forward to; the problem of the new occupant of No. 14 had been solved. Winkie Speight was coming out and Dorothie returned to England to fetch her.

Very little is known about Winkie or her family, not even her full name. From Dorothie's letters it can be ascertained that her father was a colonel and Dr Jellett knew the family. He had recommended her to the countess and Winkie had spent some months as a 'scullion' in the kitchens of Newnham Paddox, but it is apparent that her family was on a similar social level to the Denbighs. All her family, including two pretty sisters, one of whom was Winkie's twin, saw her off at Folkestone with great excitement.

Winkie's presence brought Dorothie great comfort and companionship. She was well educated, spoke French, and, most important for Dorothie, she was cheerful, witty, energetic, interested in everything and got on with everyone. Winkie became the female companion that Dorothie had lacked since she had first arrived in Flanders. Dorothie told her mother:

It is so nice having her here – I used to get just too horribly lonely here alone with old Jelly – all we have in common takes a cubic inch of space.

It was a thing one just had to put up with – & I didnt realised how hard it was to do it – until now there is someone of my own age & kind. She will be a nice 'comfortable' companion Winkie & she seems delighted to be here too – I dont ever mind an atom now it is quieting down again & things are much as when I left.

Winkie at least is like Mairi Chisholm one of the people who will never 'hurt' or 'gorry' if one does not always want to be tin tacked to them – but that equally you can frivvle & chatter with when you want to.

[20 July 1916]

Winkie was quickly introduced to Esther and soon settled down to work in the Refugee centre. Esther was also delighted at getting the extra help as there was a huge amount of work to be done. In her spare hours during the next few weeks Winkie was introduced to all Dorothie's friends and companions and taken to all her favourite places where she went for some peace and quiet. 'Took Winkie down in the evening to show her the voisinage & went for a long walk down the beach – A glorious evening & pretty Flemish lights – the only redeeming feature in a godforsaken country.'

Dorothie's return delighted Héléne, who Dorothie reported had grown so fat that she could hardly fit through the dining room door, and that the garden was looking very nice with lots of sweet peas out. She sent her mother a sample. In her absence

Dr Jellett had made a wonderful work of art, for which Dorothie was full of admiration: 'He turned an old ambulance into a modern semi-wagonette–semi-lorry – every stitch of which he made himself. The result is a collection of devices that would rejoice the heart of Heath Robinson. Considering it was all made of nothing in the back yard, it's dashed fine!'

On the whole things were good, but now it was Dorothie's turn to worry about Dr Jellett. 'Jelly is well but rather on edge. He wants a change & some leave away I think.' He was just as liable to feel stress and sadness over the constant death and destruction and he had a wife and family at home he not seen for some time. Dorothie understood. 'Our people have had a good lot of work while I was away but being by myself – it's all the months of war leaving so little time to oneself that takes it out of you.'

Back with her contacts she was able to update her father with the current situation.

I saw the General yesterday – he is not moving for the present as far as he knows of which I am very glad.

Burbidge just came back from a little excursion ½ way down English lines with Mother – Very pleased because he says they let him work in peace & he didnt get it back in the appalling way he does up here.

Big 'Charles' has been going too but not at the place you think – He makes a great noise & I trust teases them in no small measure.

The sailors are all very well as are also our people – Lots of improvements in gardens & dwellings – looks as if everyone was settling down for the rest of their natural lives to this existence.

Good accounts of the push from further down – H.O. says the French very pleased indeed with the result because it is very steady & methodical & they have made as many prisoners already as they have lost casualties, which is rather wonderful isnt it.

[22 July 1916]

The countess was probably relieved that Dorothie sounded so happy and that Winkie was proving to be a perfect companion to her daughter, however she may have slightly concerned about their diet.

Winkie has eaten 32 crystalised apricots & will soon – quite soon – be sick – Jelly on the other side is correcting proofs about female livers, full of the most revolting picture of stout ladies mit corns on their appendixes.

So doubtless I shall too be sick shortly.

Cant think of anything of the least interest to say, hence this palpitating information.

[Written by Winkie]

My dear Commandant – I hope you are as in the pink as it leaves me though whether it will continue for long I cannot say as I have partaken largely of apricots which Meestrés Diddles or Jelly will eat so in the Richness of their heart they presented them to me.

Harry's got an awful book full of the female liver or something equally beastly (I just found Diddles has said all this) This is a topping place & I feel as if it was living in a blooming cinema show all day. My neck has fairly got the crick from looking at planes.

Best love from your one time scullion, now a flea bitten Canteen Worker.

Winkie

The Damn [censored] Mosquittoes haven't left an inch of my face 'au naturel'.

Now I can go on – Yes, Winkie is a priceless sight – There is a mosquito plague on here, & she looks just like a 'Baby Maud' come over with a rash.

I took her down to see Teck to-day & she resisted as she says she was sure he would think she was always flea bitten!

To her great relief he was out. I too am devoured & the mild itches I used to indulge in at meals at N.P. that distressed Matron so – just aren't in the show at all.

[23 July 1916]

The countess might also have been amused that Winkie's spelling and her dietary habits were as bad as her daughter's, but pleased that Dorothie sounded more like her old self.

Another friend who came was Mairi Chisholm with interesting news.

Marie came in to brekker to-day looking a great duck – She is a clean child – Took years off Jelly's life by telling him that Baronne 3rd Class or Mrs Knockers is coming to take a house in our town near No 14! – Sensation as I foresee her living on our doorstep with a train of lousy Belgians avec.

I'm told Somme very active again & that we are doing very well which is good. Things not much changed here.

The Somme was certainly very active. On 26 July, 'A man from the Somme just been in – says it's very slow work & costing us very heavy casualties – I suppose it's to be expected.' There were indeed many casualties. The Battle of the Somme took place between 1 July and 18 November 1916 and was one of the largest in the Great War, indeed, one of the bloodiest battles in human history. More than 1,000,000 men were wounded or killed. British casualties on the first day were the highest in the history of the British Army – 57,470 – 19,240 of whom were killed. The huge losses forced Lord Kitchener to introduce conscription. The loss of life was not balanced by any gains for either participant. The situation was still stalemate.

Back at No. 14, Dr Jellett's behaviour was causing comment. 'Jelly has been in the sulks all day because Winkie hard-boiled his egg for breakfast – He really is an awful fool & very unbearable to associate with when he has these 'gorry' fits – & they are becoming more frequent every day alas. I doubt not but that one of us will go mad shortly!' He was probably behaving in this way for several reasons, tiredness, stress and missing his family, but unlike Dorothie, was unable to hide his unhappiness. What may have made it worse was that there were now four women living in No. 14 who got on with each other very well. The relationship between Dorothie and Winkie may have annoyed him because of their sense of humour, which he did not share, and whereas Hélène did not take offence if he ranted at her, Winkie would have answered him back. The arrival of Burbidge, Ginger, and Deb one evening to meet Winkie would not have improved his temper.

He may also have been concerned about the situation in Ireland. Following the Easter Uprising in April 1916 the revolutionaries were continuing to disturb the peace. Dorothie rarely made harsh remarks, but commenting on the damage that may have occurred from Zeppelins making their way to England she suggested, 'They might do worse than go & bomb Ireland a bit – Do it a lot of good.' As her father also held a title in the Irish aristocracy this remark sounds spiteful – not one of Dorothie's kindest reflections.

In August, a few days passed uninterrupted by shells and snipers – a chance to indulge in a rather unhealthy diet:

Mother dearest, I've just eaten a vast egg and some chocolate creams for brekker and somehow the two don't mix and am feeling ghastly sick. I feel nothing but a bomb would bring me back to my normal state. My tummy feels under my armpits and I wouldn't be surprised if winky had to operate – God help me.

[1 August 1916]

Domestic problems:

Mother dearest – Do you love me? enough to give me anything I mean? Because while I was away the few remaining face cloths fell into bits in my absence & were annexed by Jelly and Hélène as a dishcloth and motor rags. They were originally some old worn out ones I had been sent – so when you were doing linen & come upon a few holey old ones too far gone to mend – don't give them to poor Sister but send them to me to use & she and I will both be delighted

[2 August 1916]

And general news:

All sorts of excitements here yesterday – George & P of Wales came up to spend day with Teck to inspect the sailors & give the Bloke, Burbidge Deb & Ginger their medals that they hadn't had yet at B. Palace – It was a very fine affair & all the men mustered in a little review looked very pleased with themselves – Teck had given me special permission to come which was nice of him as I was the only non official onlooker – George came & spoke to me very nicely & said some kind things about my work & my being a good girl & about Da too.

Also Ld Stamfordham & Sir Dan Keppel came up & talked about Da. The former is a nice soul.

Altogether a great show & Fritz never threw anything at anyone which was rather disappointing – It would have caused a great sensation to have had a proj. In the middle of the tea party wouldn't it?

Then I was taken up to dine with the sailors – Its only the second time since Xmas I've done so, so I was made to come in honour of the new buttons.

Burbidge is going to pawn his to buy a new house!

Despite all the excitement and the pleasure of having Winkie to make her laugh, Dr Jellett's behaviour was become seriously worrying:

Jelly is awfully cantankerous these days & is really very hard to get on with – He is half thinking of giving up this work & returning to his hospital – Dont say anything about it please as he may not – But if he does I am not at all sure it wouldnt be for the best for divers reasons.

I can always go on digging here with Esther & Winkie & working with our people in the day time – As regards my safety – it wouldnt be any worse & it would make for more peace generally. Even Winkie who knows the old man well & like myself for auld lang syne & gratitude <u>will stand a great deal</u> – is beginning to find it rather trying.

This is only to say that if he should write to you he has decided to return – do not be alarmed & I think all things considered it would be wisest not to ask him to reconsider his decision – but let him go back.

... Winkie & I could perfectly well go on here without him – I know Jelly thinks we cant, but I equally know perfectly well I can.

Dorothie wrote this letter on 4 August – the second anniversary of the war. She felt despondent and told her mother that the end seemed as far away as ever. To add to this, she had just heard that General Hély d'Oissel was under orders to leave the next Sunday as he had been given an important commission elsewhere. 'It is too sad, he is such a dear & has been so very kind to me out here – I shall miss him tremendously.' And all the time she was still collecting the wounded soldiers. 'Went many miles to & fro with my ambulance to-day & swallowed much dust – I feel kind of clogged & my brain is foggy in consequence.'

But there was always something to lift her spirits. In her letter to her 'Da dear', Dorothie passed on an anecdote from the General:

The Gen told me a funny yarn yesterday. It appears down at the base town some 20 miles away a large consignment of 300 tommies arrived on the beach in lorries – They were lined up very smartly opposite the villas by the C.O. & all the local lovely ladies scenting a revue of the 'beaux anglais' dashed out in full strength. But the C. officer merely blew a whistle & before you could say knife – there were 300 tommies starkers in a row, waiting for the next whistle to march solemnly into the sea. There was a yell & a shriek from all the fair ladies who then seized their babies & belongings & fled scandalised to their houses – 'The English really are a curious race' the General added thoughtfully – 'We Frenchmen would have chosen a spot up the beach not in front of the town!'

[4 August 1916]

Dorothie's mind was so taken up with war and life in Flanders that she could not remember the date of her mother's birthday. She offered to send her the only thing she had, which was a tin of salmon, and she suggested her mother could make it into a pendant. On a more serious note, she told her mother her one wish for her was

… that next birthday will see you a little happier & your own at home again with this ghastly shadow of the war lifted at last.

For those whom God keeps in the shadow with him we must just always keep the same places for them in our hearts & that won't be very hard will it with our Hughie – There is nothing but love & goodness & happiness to remember him by – & that is what he would wish.

Your very loving Diddles – Je t'aime – tu sais?

[5 August 1916]

Dorothie did send a card. 'Mother mine, isn't this a lovely sheet of paper. It's due to two reasons. 1st it's your birthday & 2nd that Jelly has been talking hot air at me for an hour & as I wasn't listening to a word he said had lots of opportunity to draw you pretty picceys.'

The smell and noise of war was often described by Dorothie in the most original way. Nieuwpoort has been heavily shelled on 26 July but there was more noise than damage. 'It was a very sultry day & smells hung long – The place up there smelt like a classroom at school after a chemistry experiment!'

Added to the list of nuisances were the ever-present fleas. Charles the dog had picked up fleas from Lizzie, his 'lady friend up the road' who was 'crawling' with them. Dorothie washed him but he went straight back and came home re-infested. Dorothie admits to giving him a whack but was rewarded with a flea bite. Charles looked repentant but sat under a chair with a 'next time' expression on his face.

More enjoyment was taking Winkie everywhere, who was thoroughly entering into all and meeting everyone Dorothie loved and admired:

There was a very pretty little revue in the sands to-day & the general invited Winkie & me to go & see it – She hadn't seen one before & was duly thrilled – I showed her my beloved marins & all the real celebrities. It was a lovely sunny morning & really very pretty sight. I am glad she saw one.

A general giving of decorations at the end & much huggings to be done by the general of hairy old Colonels & people – I was darn glad I hadn't got to do it.

[28 July 1916]

Afterwards they went for a walk further down the Belgian lines. It was peaceful, 'all beautifully quiet & fields of poppies & cornflowers waving in the sunlight – The war didn't seem very close – on quiet days the nearer you get to Fritz the further away it all seems'.

One of the reasons Dorothie liked Winkie was her positive approach to life. As she had to work with refugees Winkie decided to learn to speak Flemish.

> Winkie is becoming a great flam scholar – She takes daily lessons with the little nuns & sits making uncouth noises, a cross between a hiccup & a snort & then informs us it is flam for 'pass the butter Miss' – Hélène anyhow is duly impressed even if we are not! ... We have been sitting in the garden quite late – & now Winkie is sitting opposite me writing Flemish verbs out of a grammar & it is nearly more than I can bear.
>
> [29 July 1916]

Dorothie did not have to settle any arguments. Esther and Winkie got on splendidly, so after the stress of facing danger and dealing with the wounded No. 14 was a cheerful place to come back to.

Friends 'blew in' regularly to enjoy the fun and check on Winkie's progress in 'Flam'. Halahan was a frequent visitor who brought news in of any naval action. The Denbighs were aware that there had been criticism about the part Hugh's squadron played in the Battle of Jutland and there were divided opinions on their action. This was distressing for the family and Dorothie wanted to confirm that the Squadron's actions and Hugh's death were not wasted:

> I wanted to ask him about the Fleet action & hadn't wanted to with everyone around so hadn't had a chance before – He had heard from different sailors, all saying how unfair the dispatch had been to Robert's Squadron & he had also seen several people who had been in the action – They all ... endorsed what Callaghan said so forcibly to Da about it.
>
> So there is no doubt at all the good their sacrifice did to the other ships & that all helps doesn't it – because one knows how proud & glad every man of them would have been to know what the fleet thinks of them.

Dorothie asked her mother to send her some memorial cards about Hugh for her to give Hély d'Oissel and the sailors who had known her brother well. They would all have agreed that the sacrifice was noble and useful.

Winkie's depiction of her job were just as colourful as Dorothie' portrayal of life at the Front.

> Winkie gives very funny accounts of her medical advice she is always being asked to give to divers old ladies of the place who come to Esther's canteen. One yesterday arrived with a quite un-mentionable foot – when asked why the Hell she didn't wash – said the apothecary had told her 3 months ago, she must on no account let water come near it – Judging by the result at present day, she had obeyed his instructions carefully!
>
> Another hysterical old lady came & said she was sure she was dying – Winkie with much pomp gave her a packet of plain

peppermint lozenges telling her to take one twenty minutes after meals – The old soul is completely happy & now cured it appears! – being convinced les 'dames anglaise' had given her a wonderful drug – Such is life.

[9 August 1916]

There was probably a sigh of relief when Dr Jellett announced that he was taking leave for ten days from 23 August. Dorothie decided to take leave at the same time, knowing she could leave Winkie in charge of No. 14 and although everyone would miss Dorothie, Winkie would be a welcoming hostess for those who wished for some light-hearted conversation and a break from the war.

Elsie Knocker also often hosted suppers, but was not quite as popular as Dorothie.

Last night Burbidge came to supper – It was rather comic – He & the Bloke had been invited to dine with the Baroness K – They looked in here on the way by, & Burbidge who hates dining out except here where he can do what he likes, felt his courage oozing out of his boots – he then firmly refused to be dragged to the sacrifice & invited himself to supper & sent the Bloke on alone!

[11 August 1916]

This does not reflect too well on Dorothie – it smacks of one-upmanship. She never admitted that she disliked Elsie Knocker, but there are occasions when her behaviour indicates that she did. It would have been more noble to have encouraged Burbidge to go to supper with Elsie. And despite her brush with Fitzpatrick in 1914 when trying to visit Rollo, she still broke the rules when it suited her.

> ... also had Thérèse de Broqueville here for 2 days & a night to see Robert.
>
> As an officer's wife he is not allowed to have her up here – So I asked him to dine with me, & never told his C.O. she was here – Then at 10 pm we rang up – brazenly told him the car was broken down & he couldn't get back till next day!!!
>
> Pure lies.
>
> [10/16 September 1916]

However, her bravery and courage were admired and unquestioned and during her leave she received her third medal of the war. It was the Military Medal, and she was the first British woman to receive it. It was awarded solely for acts of bravery under fire. She had been recommended for this medal by her friend Halahan, who had written to the Prince of Teck: 'Sir, I have the honour to submit for your consideration the services by Lady Dorothie Feilding to the unit under my command, with a view to their adequate recognition.'

On 16 December 1916 Dorothie was accompanied by her father to Windsor Castle where King George presented the medal. They were shown to a small anteroom where they chatted with Sir Harry Lloyd Verney, the groom of the chamber to the king, who explained that the king would just pin the medal on her coat. He assured her that it would do no damage. He was silenced by Dorothie's blithe response that it did not matter anyway as the coat was an old one of Moll's and she had just borrowed it. George V may have overheard this as the king was a friend of the family; he was well aware of Dorothie's disregard of material things, but he knew she would value the medal.

On her return she was delighted that her other friends Deb and Ginger had also been awarded the Crosse de Guerre for 'helping put out fire in the French gun pit, while the ammunition was going off. This gun was close to theirs & being heavily strafed' and that 'Winkie is full of bounce & sends her love'.

The weather was awful, 'such a gale of rain, got soaked this afternoon', and badly injured soldiers needed moving from Nieuwpoort to Dunkirk. But meeting old friends cheered her up, as always. 'Was distributing cigs to the poor blessés down there when a festive Marin in the corner shrieked out "Mees Dorothié" & I discovered an old friend who swore he had known me since Ghent. We parted the best of friends & he the better off for baccy!'

There were always concerts the inhabitants of No. 14 could attend. Perhaps it was just the joy of being with people she liked, and on occasions her humour is schoolgirlish:

Winkie, Jelly and I were invited to a concert show the french soldiers got up – No end of a hurush & Albert & Elizabeth of Belgium & millions of fat old generals – The latter behind whom we were sitting gave us giggles – Rows of shiny bald heads beating time to the music! A lady pal of Jelly's asked me fatuously what my medals were for. I assured her one was for putting out a fire in the back garden and the other – another fire in the backyard. 'How very interesting', she replied, 'do you know Lady Dorothie, I tried to put out a little fire at our hospital but wasn't so fortunate the other day.' I remained maturely solemn and had the idea – must really write a pamphlet on Fire Brigades. I think now my fame is sure to spread! Ha ha!

[14 September 1916]

Or perhaps it was simply the chance to feel life was normal for a few hours as the war took its toll.

You should have seen my poor old ambulance last night! The contents were me – Jelly – two light blessés – 2 malades – 2 brancardies [brancardiers, stretcher-bearers] – two enormous tin cases for the hospital place, an officers luggage and aumoneirs [aumônières] orderly and a damaged bicycle. I'm stinking of petrol and have just been removing the motor oil from the British warms and the overalls in the house – no mean job – have had a lot to do since I've been back in the way of taking blessés more than before I went away also divers are the gadgets on the tapis.

[19 September 1916]

No. 14 was becoming something of a palace. Dorothie had described in an earlier letter the curtains and decorations she had put in and described the cellar as a baronial hall, but the house was to be improved.

The Canadians offered to build me a fire-place in the sitting room, as we haven't one in the whole house – only a dirty little stove – The trouble was how to get a barrel of cement – ½ a ton into the house without the old 'Patron' next door who owns

14 butting in & raising Hell – as he always does if he even hears you driving a nail in the wall.

Of course he came in like a jack in the box the moment they arrived, but Hélène informed him gravely we were making a 'trou-de-couchon – a pigsty in the back garden – He quite believed it & asked what we were going to feed them on!

Thus the fire place was well underway & a nice large hole knocked in his ceiling before he could interfere, so we are the proud possessors of a nice open fire place – The only trouble is that there is hardly any room left to sit in, but you cant have everything can you?

[29 September 1916]

'Just like Frankton' – referring to a house in Frankton village owned by the Denbighs.

If there was less room to sit in, it would not have troubled those who frequently 'blew in' to enjoy the ladies' company and share a pleasant meal. They also had to put up with unwelcome visitors – fleas this time.

> A plague of fleas has come upon us with these sunny days & we had a great 'swat' party this morning with brooms, squashing them on the ceiling, where they made beastly goo marks – Charles barking madly with excitement & devouring the corpses as they fell – he swears you cannot beat them as an hors d'oeuvre.
>
> [1 October 1916]

Possibly during these visits by calling in at Mission Headquarters she obtained the latest information on the war.

Dorothie and Charles resting against a haycock.

I hear our losses these last 10 days good ... wonderfully few considering, & far less than in the earlier stages. The artillery preparation seems to have been stupendous – I have seen several people these last days who have just left there – The French have only a little over a quarter of our losses from last July – I have this from the old boy you & Squeaker stayed with out here – Partly due to their more efficient artillery preparations & a great deal because the Germans have massed many more troops in front of the English – They would rather go back 10 miles in front of the French than in front of us as everyone knows – But everything seems going really well now & generally pretty optimistic about Fritz being made to draw back in the S to his 2nd line before the winter. I'm afraid no earthly chance of that here – The coast is too precious to them, & they will have to be very beat indeed before they will let go of it.

[29 September 1916]

Dorothie was also aware that Zeppelins were appearing in the skies over England and the earl had written to tell her about his experience.

How exciting for you coming in for the Zep Fluff at Brentwood – I guessed you would have been dancing around in pyjamas squashing slugs with your bare toes & yelling like mad & see my surmise was correct – Haven't yet had Taffys account of it – I heard a funny account of the Zep at Colchester tho' probably you've heard it too, of how the Boch C.O. came & asked the owner of a small cottage 50 yds away from where he landed, where he could telephone etc. It was a lonely part & the man naturally wanted to get rid of the Boche & his crew so started telling him the way to C__ The Boche replied 'Damm you I know that – I know Colchester a ruddy site better than you do' – There's organisation for you!

[1 October 1916]

The family had not stopped thinking about Hugh and were evidently still troubled that the *Defence's* action was still being debated.

I am so glad you saw Beatty & Chalmers & that you would hear things 1st hand from them – Every sailor I have come across since says how gallantly the little Defence fought & attacked & it all helps doesnt it.

Chalmers knew Hughie & had been shipmates with him a good time ago – He was also a friend of Jack Hanleys. I still find myself all the time Da dear thinking of Hughie as if he was at sea & of all sorts of things to tell him – He still seems to come into everything so very much, that at times it just seems an awful dream, that he will come back to us.

[1 October 1916]

Other losses served to sadden Dorothie and increase her anxiety over Rollo:

Poor Dick Stanhope – I am so very sorry for his wife – It is tragic – The Guards lost terribly but seem to have fought superbly as always. I was much interested in your account of the tanks & then attack. I am glad Rollo is back – the

Coldstream are out of it for the time being – He's grown such a nice boy Peter this last year, & come on so in every way, don't you think so?

[1 October 1916]

She was not looking forward to her third birthday spent in Flanders. 'Birthdays are hateful things now, so full of memories of Hughie Mother dear – I hate mine.'

8

ANOTHER MEDAL
AND PROPOSALS OF
MARRIAGE – DECLINED

Dorothie's twenty-sixth birthday proved to be quite eventful. First, she received 'another £50 – that makes £200 & 2 ambulances I've got in a week – call that nuffink?' Second, the Germans started an attack from which Dorothie had a lucky escape and third, she had a visitor.

Fritz started & looked like attacking, so we gave him hell & then he did give us hell – & so the world keeps going round & round – Dear old N__ was no health resort & we trembled for the car one time when we had left it under an arch while getting blessés at the dressing station – Two fat obus landed just on the car but luckily both duds & so nothing happened – Yesterday morning Mr Vaughan RN (who lunched at Delys with us the other day, Hughie's friend) turned up cheerfully here having got 3 days leave to spend in Flanders – so he came on the car with us, & got lots for his money so was frightfully pleased at coming in for a strafe, as are all Cooks conducted tourists! – We have given him a cabin up at our barracks.

[9 October 1916]

The next day Dorothie wrote to her mother that she had received a proposal from Mr Vaughan.

He is a very nice soul, & I like him very much, but was so sorry because before he left he asked if there would be any chance for me to marry him, & I had to say I couldn't – Poor soul, he's always had a very lonely time of it through life, & was very devoted to his gunner brother who was killed not long ago at Ypres. You remember his writing to me about it when I was home don't you? I think men are wonderfully brave sometimes at making up their minds, don't you? – Everything really is very odd these days – The days when things weren't odd seem so far away, almost like a dream.

[10 October 1916]

During the exchange of hell there were a lot of 'The more one can help them right out here at the pulse of things the more this actual work means to me – I can't describe it, but it's very real & means much to me every day somehow.'

A letter from her father made her feel 'very bucked', as he had asked Teck about coming out to Flanders to visit her.

So longing to find out what Teck thought of it, I have just rung up to ask him to dinner tomorrow – He says he'd love to come, & he added you had written him & he thought it would be managed & he's sent you a wire – Teck for ever – that really is nice of him isnt it & I am thrilled to the teeth – what fun it will be having you – & wont we raise Cain just – Things have been very gingery round here just lately, but I expect with your usual luck Fritz will retire for a weeks siesta as soon as you arrive

[11 October 1916]

Her friends were also pleased by the proposed visit. 'The Bloke thanks you for your message & sends you his love in return. The Navy will be very pleased to see you.'

On 19 October Dorothie described to her mother 'an awful afternoon'. However, it was not a result of the German attacks or injured soldiers; she had received another proposal and again, it was totally unexpected.

Mother mine –

Mr de Broqueville the father came up to see me at 14, & we had a long talk – It appears his son Pierre wants to marry me awfully, & spoke to his father about it many months ago, but was told to wait a little – I dont think you ever met Pierre. He is the one in the 1st Guides Cavalerie, the very tall dark, good looking one, & was in the Army before the war – He is an awfully nice boy, but just a dear big baby – About 25 I think! But temperamentally a perfect child & I am afraid it would never be for that reason – I wouldnt marry a foreigner unless I cared very very much – I think that is essential – Pierre is a dear boy, but I really couldnt ever marry him – There is not enough in him to satisfy me I'm afraid. But the Broquevilles have been such perfect dears to me, it is awful not being able to do it, as I am afraid the father was fearfully anxious for it to be & was thinking it would be O.K. He wrote to his wife about it already in Brussels got an answer saying if he was pleased she was too, & was apparently very nice about it, which makes it all the worse – It was because he heard father was coming out here that he came up to see me because he wanted to talk it over with him if I would – I told him that I was very fond of someone who had been killed, so that in the hopes it would soften it a little & not seem ungratefully callow for all they have done for me – Will you please write to the father about it & say I told you, & thank him very much for all the care & affection he had for me – This never occurred to me – Pierre when quartered near here, often comes now & then & gives me a ride & a gee, & I considered it was good for us both to get a good healthy shake up & a change from our respective ventures which are both pretty deadly – And now everything is in the consommé!

Much love Darling,

Dodo

Fortunately, the de Broquevilles understood and continued to behave towards Dorothie as they had always done.

Robert de Broq was here yesterday afternoon & went for a stroll in the evening – The whole family have been frightfully nice to me & I am glad because it has taken away any feeling of uncomfortableness – I felt at 1st that they might think I had been playing the fool, because they so little understand abroad the way English girls are brought up to be quite natural & pals with men, & that they wd think I had meant something by seeing & being good friends with the boy – But I am glad to say there is no question of that, so I am happier about it, because they have been such dears to me all along out here – & I wd hate to hurt them in any way ... Papa Broq wrote me such a nice letter too yesterday.

[20 October 1916]

Rumours always annoyed Dorothie, some of which added to her grief. One of the generals from headquarters had been told she was engaged to Pierre de Broqueville and wanted to know if it were true. She felt sorry for Pierre because he would be embarrassed and Dorothie acidly observed that 'Foreigners are such busy-bodies'. More upsetting were the rumours and discussions concerning the Battle of Jutland and criticism concerning Warrant-Engineer Thomas H. Roberts of HMS *Defence*. Her mother also told her that she had heard Hughie had intended to leave the ship, but the family knew nothing of this. Dorothie gained some comfort from reading some articles on the subject by Rudyard Kipling, a close friend of the Feildings who had also lost a son in the war.

A wire from her father was a pleasant surprise. He was coming out in a few days. 'It will be too nice for words having him here & I am just delighted, bless him.' She also reported that her car had taken 101 wounded soldiers in one month; evidence that although there were no major battles being fought, snipers were still watching out for a careless head appearing over the edge of the trenches and shells were continually flying over and causing damage and death. Sometimes the Germans failed to cause any damage at all, just a few near misses.

There was a lot of noise up at N__ yesterday so we were out pretty late – when we got back we found that Fritz to celebrate King Albert's birthday had had a good old hate at this place for the 1st time for ever so long – He cast about 123 but as not a single person or cat was even blessed – it was rather waste of breath on his part – None anywhere near 14 – as we are right out of the shell zone ... Gurney was shook up yesterday at the dressing station – one burst alongside his car & large lumps buzzed by over his steering wheel which did nothing beyond making him sit up.

[16 November 1916]

But there were other occasions when the damage caused suffering to the few inhabitants left:

Just been to see the wreck of a little cobblers house in the town here – absolutely nothing left of it – The old couple were in the tiny cellar at the time & buried under the debris & had to be dug out – This morning they were sitting in the ruins, poor old souls, shivering with cold & shock generally & half angry while they poked about hoping to find some of their belongings in the rubbish – It is so sad to see them & so pitiful.

[20 November 1916]

It was also very hard for the soldiers, though they were keeping up their morale under the most severe weather conditions.

It has got awfully cold here these last few days. The Bloke back from the Somme says obviously being in a trench up to your waist in water has its drawbacks & not to be recommended –

Awfully impressed with the moral of our infantry but say they are a bloodthirsty crowd & its extraordinary hearing them talking of things after a scrap – It takes very little to get the veneer off & down to primitive beast man, in spite of everything – doesn't it?

[16 November 1916]

There had been some successes for the Allies at Verdun and the exuberant behaviour of her second favourite regiment, the Zouaves, provided Dorothie with an extra load of work. Although very tired, she wrote to regale her mother with their activities and captured their courage in her own original way. She also described the arrival of some impressive but dangerous allies:

Yesterday the Zouaves very bucked over the Verdun successes & hung up all sorts of flags out of the trenches with insulting messages to Fritz – Result to-day the latter has been on the strafe with his 'minnies' & our people have been busy – A rather expensive joke I'm afraid.

There is an extraordinary regiment here now, composed entirely of French convicts brought back from the colonies & made to fight – They have livened up the district considerably!! When not fighting they cant be beaten & have made a great name for themselves & are always given the dirty job – But in billets they are the devil – They have slain 6 belge gendarmes, 2 old ladies & stolen innumerable hens this last week – divers of them we shot at dawn at intervals but none of the others seem the least depressed thereby.

One of their officers told me in N__ the other day that even in the trenches, no sooner is a man knocked out, than all the others are down on him like harpies to bag his watch & rifle his pockets generally.

Goodnight dear – I am sleepy tired & wish I was dead ever so much.

Yr loving Dodo

[27 October 1916]

The earl's visit was a great success. He was as popular and entertaining as his daughter.

Its so nice having Da here, & we have had huge fun, but life is simply one dam thing after another & we tore round in circles looking at everything & everybody from Huns to Albert!

Last night a great supper party at the sailors & Da sang Alouette & Bug a lou – The latter was a huge success and they loved it – Everybody loves Da – he is perfectly priceless when he gets going with an old piano!

[31 October 1916]

Dorothie was sad to see her father go. 'We had such fun together – he is such a lamb that man – everybody loves him.'

The de Broquevilles had moved to a new chateau which Dorothie described as 'awfully nice – large & more private than the old one, with a moat round it – really very snug'. The change, as always lifted her spirits: 'It is a lovely sunny morning & the colours on the trees down here are too gorgeous – I don't know why but autumn makes no difference to the drabness of Furnes – There are only poplars & the leaves just drop without changing.'

Back in Furnes, Dorothie sent her mother 'just a line to say it is a moth eaten war & I am fati – gued of it'. She told her that her friend Ginger was leaving to go to sea as the navy was short of young officers and that Deb (Caswell) would also be going soon. She commented sadly that 'Soon there will be no-one of the old Firm but me in Flanders.'

Dorothie was still responsible for finding men to drive the ambulances. 'If you hear of anyone to suit us let us know as we are hunting for a man to replace a member whose eyesight is too bad for the work out here – He can't drive at night & in the rain in the daylight.'

Dr Jellett's treatment of Kemp, a new member of the Corps, made Dorothie laugh, but on reflection seems quite hard on a young, raw recruit, unused to the war-torn areas.

… he took the new member out for a run in the car & made him drive a sort of exam – the poor new man is not a very good motorist yet, very new to it all & easily put in a fuss – So Jelly not finding the highroad interesting enough as a test, at once takes him up into N__ & up by the woods where he got proper shelled & the fear of God put in him – all this as Jelly explained carefully was 'Just to give him confidence' … Personally I think he will have many nightmares to-night instead & will probably die of fright or the palsy before morning.

[14 November 1916]

This incident had repercussions that still amused Dorothie. She wrote to her father:

Col Da dear –

I have just received a most compromising wire which will show the sort of reputation I now have: 'Lady D F etc – Beseech you return my son immediately – Kemp'.

I think it is quite priceless & so does everyone else – & I am being called a babysnatcher!! – Must have caused quite a flutter in the graph officer en route... The reason of it all is a youth called Kemp who came to replace Newall & is somewhat a rabbit – he came in for a good few obus at once & Jelly took him up to teach him how to reverse a car under heavy fire at N__ as he explained 'Just to give the lad confidence'... This put the lid on it & the lad wrote home to papa – his nerves & health wouldn't stand it hence frenzied wires from his parent birds – about 3 a day! – We explained he was under a military contract for 6 months & must stick it – He is already improved – & I think a little hard work & being shot at as often as possible will soon buck him up – Will report progress anyway! – of course he may pass away under the experiment, but as in this case 'it wouldn't really matter', that great Flanders maxim holds good.

[21 November 1916]

Dorothie was rarely angry but on 20 November she wrote home to her mother to express her fury.

Mrs Knocker has published a damnable book called 'The Cellar house of Pervyse' – Thank God she had left me out of it practically, but a lot of 'Munco' about it & people will undoubtedly associate one with that type of woman – Get it read it & see if you don't think it is the worse taste you ever saw – It makes one sick of being a woman & I am sorry she has made Mairi Chisholm look such a fool too – She should have been held under water for 48 hours when young.

[20 November 1916]

On this occasion Dorothie's ire was misplaced. The book was not written or published by Elsie Knocker, but journalist called G. E. Mitton. He wrote it at the suggestion of Major A. A. Gordon, who had witnessed the courage and devotion of Elsie Knocker and Mairi Chisolm and was full of admiration for them. He had persuaded them to entrust their journals to him and then asked Mitton to write up their story. Whilst Dorothie would have refused completely to countenance such a publication. Elise Knocker agreed because she intended to use any profits to help the soldiers.

Dorothie hated publicity and would rather have been totally omitted. She was referred to a few times, as 'Dot' Feilding, which she may have found annoying, as she was always known as Diddles or Dodo, but what really made her livid was the way Elsie, as she believed, had distorted the image of women. However, it was Mitton who should be blamed for the style of writing, which is fawning, over-effusive, and sycophantic. He portrayed the two women as angels, pure, meek, and faultless; caricatures that did not reflect the true courage and personalities of the two women, and who, like Dorothie, had been honoured with medals. However, the book was out, and Dorothie was disgusted.

Dorothie's attitude to women was remarkable. In England these were the years of the suffragist movement where women were demanding equality. In the first decade of the twentieth century the Suffragettes became politically active, demanded their right to vote and to be recognised as equal to men. Dorothie never mentioned the subject directly in her letters. Born into an aristocratic background, she clearly did not have to concern herself with freedom and equality. There seemed to be no gender problems for her to challenge within her family or among her friends. Her father and brothers, whom she adored, treated all the females in the family with great respect and equality. However, there are one or two remarks that indicate that she had an opinion on the matter and she shared her thoughts with her mother and in this letter, with her father.

The French poilu ... I was talking to one at N__ 2 days ago & he was proudly showing me the photos of his wife & family – one of the latter was a pretty little girl, so I politely complimented him on the beauty of his offspring – he merely remarked 'Et c'est bien le moins – après tous le mal qu'on doit se donner pour les faire!' [and that's the least of it, after all the trouble needed to do it]. I nearly said, 'My dear man I think your lady wife had got more to grouse about! But on 2nd thoughts decided I didn't know him well enough, so we shook hands warmly & left it at that!

[17 October 1916]

Dorothie had told her mother about George, one of the French orderlies whose wife had just given birth to a fifth baby. George wanted his five days leave.

He then explained that he had now 3 living & 2 dead & added 'Isn't it sickening those 2 died – or else I should be at the arrière'

– Because you know all French soldiers having 5 kids are now given base jobs – What amused me was his utter indifference to the kids being gone until he found it entailed his doing more work – But as he philosophically remarked with a shrug 'Que voulez vous – je n'ai pas de chance' … I expect George's wife will have to work double time now to produce twins before the war is over so that he can get a base job – Votes for women!

[8 February 1916]

But rather than publicly demand equality, Dorothie's approach to women's relationships with men was subtle. She understood that a successful outcome to any differences was that both sides felt they had gained something. She was a good mediator and advisor, persuasive rather demanding. She agreed with her mother's analysis of an historical female figure:

I think your view of Lady Hamilton was quite right – I think women if they wish can keep men very often by using their influence in the right way – At least I know in several cases I have been able to help men over stiles in their lives, where if they hadn't been fond of me they would have taken the wrong road – I remember many years ago you telling me 'It can never hurt a man to care for a good woman' – & I have often thought of it since & it has helped me to do the right thing by people – I know if a man looks up to you he will unconsciously almost do the best that it is in him, just because he knows it pleases you to feel he is doing so – Since the war I think women can help men in these ways & influence them more than they have ever done before.

[24 October 1916]

One of the cases was her very good friend, Henry Halahan. He told the countess that it was 'through Dorothie, whose inspiration and example he was converted to the right way'. One of the disadvantages of this approach was that on some occasions the men who she was trying to help mistook her kindness for more romantic feelings. There were probably more proposals that she had to decline, and these upset her.

Dorothie never discussed politics in her letters but her friendship with Rupert Ommanney indicates that she always sought peace and reconciliation brought about by discussion rather that belligerence; the aims of the Chatham Dining Club matched her own. Ommanney and his friend Guy Dawnay were the founders of the club in 1910. Its professed aims were:

> To bring together for the exchange of ideas of men of various professions and political creeds, who are anxious to overcome the obstacles in the way of the effective consolidation of the British Empire. To seek and examine the means by which such consolidation may be brought about.
>
> [Chatham Club Brochure 1910]

It is possible that Tom Brockholes had the same ideals and this influenced his decision to go to India the same year.

A few days after the 'damnable book' came out Dorothie had a visitor whose request did not please her.

> A funny old bird with whiskers all over his face, even round his eyes pranced in here to-day, & wanted to do a painting of me for the official French Album de Guerre, he is tolled off

for the purpose, being a distinguished artist – In addition to being in the album I was to have the great privilege to be then sold for 1d on a coloured p-card ... You will be surprised to hear I wasn't taking any, only it took me from 9 am to 10-30 to convince Whiskers that I really meant it – He thought it most odd & we actually parted with many deep bows, & expressions of mutual admiration! – I quite expect him to be in tomorrow & go thro' it all again.

[21 November 1916]

The artist may have been Charles Fouqueray, a well-known painter, and he must have been extremely surprised to have his offer rejected. But he was not aware how averse Dorothie was to publicity and after the shock of *The Cellar House of Pervyse* she was determined to avoid any invasion of her privacy.

Dorothie was used to the wounds caused by shells and bullets, but she also had to deal with other problems.

We have a lot of malade soldiers at times suffering from the acute itch, or as it is politely called in medical aids 'la gale' [scabies] – I had two of them yesterday up at N__ to take away – A Zouave standing by was awfully sick at seeing men being evacuated for so small a trouble as he considered & said 'The town I come from near Grenoble has 3,000 in habitants & over 2,000 of them have "la gale."'

I sympathised but made a mental note to keep clear of the neighbourhood of Grenoble! Squeaker would like it I feel sure – Matron would have too!!!

[25 November 1916]

Although Dorothie had lost her chance of marrying the man she loved, she was delighted for those who found a man they wanted to marry. Esther McNeil told Dorothie she had just become engaged to her cousin, Colonel McNeil. Dorothie wanted to drink their toast that evening but having no alcohol she made some Bird's custard and drank the toast with that. As the colonel was in the Sudan Cavalry Regiment, Esther was going to stay out so that she could see him regularly, a situation of which Dorothie heartily approved. Ever practical, Dorothie observed that it must be 'nice to go on being McNeil & not have to re-mark your vests & pants!'

Dorothie and Charles on their wedding day, with staff and convalescent solders at Newnham Paddox.

The book was still irritating Dorothie, and she referred to it again on 30 November.

How go things with you? I got your copy of the review of Mrs K's book last night – Reviewers are odd people, it is impossible to know what they will praise or crab – Get the book yourself and read it & tell me how it strikes you as a casual reader? I of course may be prejudiced, but the whole tone of it disgusts me.

I am going up to see Mairi Chisholm to-day, so will see what she thinks of it.

Despite these irritations the last few letters of 1916 capture some of the breezy spirit of her early letters in 1914. She was delighted that her mother was 'fed up with Mrs K's book', and she was looking forward to spending her third Christmas of the war at home at Newnham Paddox with her family.

9

ANOTHER PROPOSAL –
ACCEPTED

When Dorothie returned to No. 14 on 5 January, she found Winkie had been suffering from 'flu, and was now going home for a few days to her twin's wedding. Mrs Taylor was still very ill so Dorothie took on Winkie's job, which included 'cutting 450 treacle sandwiches & getting the kids' dinners – Treacle days are a joy of stick as you can imagine!' It was also very cold. The winter of 1917 was the worst that Europe has seen for many years. The soldiers suffered badly from frostbite and exposure, some of them losing fingers and toes. The trenches did little to provide shelter or warmth and at night clothes and blankets froze solid. Food and drink also froze and made it nearly impossible for the solders to eat regularly. Dorothie wondered 'how snowy places like the Vosges compare with these flat muddy countries as regards discomfort for the men in the trenches'. The cold also affected the vehicles. 'Such hard frost here & we are all having awful trouble to stop cars freezing up – However much you empty the radiator there is always a small deceptive bit of water lurking in some bit of the pipe that succeeds in freezing up …' The weather was affecting the support workers. For two days and nights torrents of rain fell and turned everything into a sea of mud – the notorious mud of Flanders. Dorothie told her father:

The roads are in a grand state of old slop – In fact Flanders in top winter form – I am working double time these days as I do cantine from brekker to lunch for Winkie so that she could slip back for a few days for her twin's wedding in London – Then in the afternoons we go down to the far off hospital near the base practically every day now & dont get in till after dark – There is nothing very new or exciting to tell you – Been one or 2 little hates up at N__ since I've been back. My friends the convict regiment seemed to have quieted down & not committed any enormities lately which is dull of them – They are leaving too which is sad.

[10 January 1917]

Another friend was also ill:

Poor little Burbidge down with appendicitis which is sickening for him – He is down at the Base Hospital but they hope by starving him to get him over to Blighty in a few days to get him operated on there instead of here – The Bloke & he very sick – as they are afraid someone might get sent out here instead of him if he takes a long time getting well – I hope he doesn't get moved – It would be sickening.

[15 January 1917]

At least there were the suppers where Dorothie and her friends could keep warm and, on occasions, be entertained by the most interesting new arrivals for the navy.

> There is a sailor – one Adams – now with them who is one of the corniest cusses I've ever met – A rough diamond who has done everything from Navy to S. Pole with Shackleton, then chucked Navy & did absolutely everything for a few years & joined Territ artillery (Lord Fitzwilliams) at beginning of war – Got awfully bored with them all so just got into a train, went away to Admiral Hood at Dover & joined up with him in the Navy again – The Gunners want to courtmartial him for desertion after the war! – But he tells the most priceless yarns in quite the funniest & most solemn way – All the others love him & last night I laughed so much, I couldn't manage to do any eating & I nearly choked whenever I tried – He's a great asset to the stagnation of Flanders.
>
> [23 January 1917]

Adams was Jameson Adams, the Antarctic explorer who was a member of the Nimrod Expedition, the first expedition led by Ernest Shackleton in an unsuccessful attempt to reach the South Pole. He was recalled to the navy at the outbreak of war and became Flag Lieutenant to Admiral Hood commanding the Dover Patrol. Then, after a period of special work at the Ministry of Munitions, he was posted to Flanders to command a battery of naval siege guns. He was just the sort of man whose adventurous spirit and frequent brushes with authority would appeal to Dorothie.

JAMESON BOYD ADAMS
1908

Sir Jameson Boyd
Adams KCVO CBE
DSO RD was a British
Antarctic explorer and
Royal Naval Reserve
officer.

By 29 January the weather was still causing problems and Dorothie was cross with herself. She was an excellent horsewoman, driver and motor mechanic and a very good nurse, but she found that she could not skate and it frustrated her.

My fingers are frozen absolutely stiff & I cannot write you a sparkling letter in consequence for I am much too cross ... All the canals here are frozen the most amazing thickness & I go sliding in the evenings when we come in, until the ends of my toes are all blistered – I shall have to give over for a day or two – It annoys me when I slide 10 yds & sit down hard, to see a tiny Flam in sabots slide some 500 yds all out ...

The ice was a problem the Germans attempted to use to their advantage.

The most tremendous heavy firing last night, & we were afraid it was the Boche making a stunt across the ice as the inundations are of course frozen – However they keep it broken every day with field guns – enough to stop any serious advance over it – The noise turned out to be of the Belgians making however as they were ousting Fritz from a forward position you saw in the communiqué we had captured a few days ago – We had practically no casualties tho' the noise was terrific – of course at night things always sound exaggerated & the flash of guns make everything light up ... I've just been talking to Mairi Chisholm whose farm is close by there & she says the old house was proper on the shake all night from the firing – So was No. 14 – Its awfully odd the way sound carries further inside a house – I mean often here when there is heavy firing going on a long way away – 30 miles or so – you hear & feel it awfully plainly in the house – You then go outside to listen & you can hear nothing.

[31 January 1917]

Dorothie got away from the noise for two days with Rollo, staying in Boulogne with a friend. The return journey lived up to Dorothie's standard of danger and adventure. 'The snow had come down very heavily in the night & where it had been swept on the hills had just become a sheet of ice & the car wheels couldn't grip – Eventually whenever we stuck, beseeching the aid of any passing members of the British Army, I persuaded them to help push the pram up the hills.'

When they returned home Dorothie accused the inhabitants of No. 14 of kindly handing her 'a few microbes as to-day I have a dirty cough & a throat & am feeling fed up & most shop soiled'. She also commented that she had timed her return just right; the noise was still in evidence and her skills were needed:

… yesterday Tues we had a strafe on here up at N__ no end of a tea party, artillery & infantry. All our cars were on the road all day, & we only got in late so I hadnt time to write to Mother – Praps you will please send this on to her – The post is bad here as everywhere & been to below zero often lately at nights – Even the edges of the sea are frozen which I believe hardly ever happens – I didnt know it ever did anywhere near England or France – The bombing season is quite over here now I am glad to say & I have invested in another 7 francs worth of glass for my bedroom window which bores me. The place here where we keep our reserve cars had the door knocked cockeyed by the explosion of one – Last time they shelled one hit the next house to the garage some 10 yds away, so our cars seem lucky – Nothing ever comes near No. 14 so you mustn't be fussed.

[7 February 1917]

On 23 February Dorothie sent a postcard to her father telling him that she was off on 15 days leave to see Marjie and was 'thrilled to the teeth – It will be joyous to have something different & really nice to look at'. Marjie's husband Dudley had suffered from head injuries and been captured. He was later exchanged for some German prisoners and sent to a hospital in neutral Switzerland where he remained until the

Armistice. Marjie had gone out to stay so she could be with him and keep up his spirits.

Surprisingly, Dorothie's next letter was six weeks later, on 30 March when she had just arrived in Chateau d'Oex, Switzerland. Dorothie reported that she was having great fun and the change of air and circumstances was very beneficial for her.

We had a joyous day & only got in at 8-30 – A really lovely little valley & God sent day – The sun set on the mountains was a dream – All the snow lit up with orange pink lights – In fact the nicest day I've spent for many months – Really lovely things to look at on all sides, which made one feel good inside.

Quite a lot of wild flowers down there as the valley being wider then here gets more sun – Crowds of 'snow-flakes' Fat snowdrops with yellow patches – I enclose you one to see.

[4 April]

The weather held up:

I just loved a real rest in getting right away from war & hospital things for the 1st time for over a year – The country is perfectly gorgeous there after the monotony & dreariness of these everlasting plains. I had some fine weather there & some snowy days, but enjoyed them all

[10 April]

She was able to report to the mother that Marjie was much better than Dorothie had seen her look for three or four years, 'more like her old self & fatter, not such a run down little rake'.

Dorothie, as usual, obtained the clinical details of Dudley's condition:

I thought his skull had been chipped – It apparently never was but the bullet depressed the skull with a result it presses slightly on the brain – This gives him often headaches & general mental depression – Then if he takes any violent exercise, or overtaxes his brain, the blood pressure resulting increases the pressure of the brain on the skull & gives him bad heads. The specialist at Montreux has dieted him etc & says to give it a good chance to respond to treatment as he hopes the brain may adapt itself in time to the skull pressure & cease to react. If this doesn't happen later on when he returns to England he may have to be trepanned & the skull raised.

Meanwhile there is nothing for him to do but wait – He is pretty fit himself – The chief trouble is he gets so awfully sick of this little place, since he is cooped up & has nothing to do – I think England would of course cure him quicker than anything – Generally speaking he is much better than I expected to find him. Its the fact he gets so bored … here in the endless days with nothing to do, which is the worst for him.

The problem of his just waiting and having nothing to do was partly because he was under Swiss medical authorities, which Dorothie, with her usual insight, criticised sharply.

The Swiss are swines to the men here – our Govt pay them for hospital treatment of the men – The Swiss just herd them into a big building, feed them abominably, give them the minimum of doctoring, & absolutely no nursing or care – Not even a single nurse or orderly or attendant in the whole building – The men just look after each other & everything is beastly – some of the men go for 2 & 3 weeks without having their beds turned or made – All the officers wives here imploring to be allowed in as V.A.D.'s to run the place & look after the men, but the Swiss won't hear of it – They arent even allowed to visit the men there – The reason is the Swiss doctors bag half the money for themselves that should be spent on the men & dont want to be interfered with – I cant tell you what a revelation it is to me – I thought they were as well looked after as at home.

[30 March 1917]

Dorothie arrived back in Flanders on 10 April and supplied her mother with the details of her journey home, which, as usual with Dorothie, was full of incident.

I got back here O.K. after the most awful journey from Switzerland – It takes 3 days each way from here to Chateau d'oex. I was lucky enough to get a lift back from Paris in a little Belgian lady's car – on the way we stopped at Amiens to lunch with Belge Grison of the big nose – Evys pal who has been to N.P. – Walking thro' the restaurant there was suddenly a yell & my arm was grabbed by someone at a table who turned out to be Peter in there for a 24 hrs jolly for Easter – Sensation! – So I went & lunched with him & we had huge fun – He is out of the line for the moment making roads & being due for 3 or 4 days Paris leave – is coming to spend them with me here instead … He is one of the few members of my family who have never visited the 'chateau Mees' at No. 14 – It will be great fun …

I had the strangest journey coming back from Switzerland – Even more of a scrum that going down – One had to change about 8 times from Chateau d'oex to Paris & never gets any sleep as all through the night you have to keep climbing out of trains & waiting hours for the next – At Dijon I had to wait 3 hrs on the platform at 1 a.m. – A seething mass of soldiers returning from leave everywhere so nowhere for a nit to wriggle even on the platform, whereas all waiting rooms out of the question – Getting weary I proceeded to sit on my suit-case in the middle of the mob. In the dark a fat French tommy some 3 yds square falls right over me & nearly squashes me flat & leaves me for dead – He got up & said 'Mon Dieu, et j'ai presque éciasé la pauvre petite bète!' & proceeded to pick me up & apologise & we parted the best of friends – Of course no sooner had I sat down again than someone else fell over me, so I gave it up! – I shared supper with a nice little Zouave who hadnt any, & the dear thing in consequence carted my suit-case for me for the rest of the journey & so it was a true case of head upon the waters – He had come from St Quentin & had a hectic time of it.

At last a train arrived & we got off, all the places full of course – Then arrived 3 tommies & said they were permissionaries & might they squeeze in too – so they did – But they then saw their pals George & Joseph & Alfonse & Jules & Robert & le Sergeant on the platform & brought all of them in too. Then Alfonse & Jules & the Sergeant sat on me & proceeded to have supper – Alfonse was the underneathest but one (which was me) & proceeded to try & extricate a string of sausages from his pocket – The sort like they have here – Greenish sausages on a string & each sausage tied round &

wound with the string too – I suppose to try & localise the explosion – of course Alfonse was so squashed he couldnt get the sausage out of his pocket & everyone had to come & so a tug of war – At last it came out with a rush & was cut up & distributed – I was offered some & had to think of all sorts of reasons as to why I couldnt eat sausage so as not to hurt their feelings – An old French lady in the carriage was very stuffy & scornful about it!

Of course at least ½ of the Company were genteely tight – It's the 1st time in my life I have seen anyone tight & was not disgusted – Here were these poor devils, all going back to Verdun & all good soldiers & pals & just been spending their leave as they like – after all there was no merit in me not being tight, just because I hate it – My form of leave was to see my family & see something lovely & mountains – Theirs was to see their families & have a drink – after all we each had what we were hankering for hadnt we? – Why should I have it & not they?

Back in Furnes the weather had not improved and was bitterly cold with sleet and hail most days. Dorothie was disappointed that Peter did not manage to visit. She dined with the Prince of Teck and heard that although the allies had made a good advance there had been some terribly hard fighting and there had been many wounded to collect. Dorothie was soon back at work, on 15 April in Nieuwpoort, which was seeing a lot of activity. She had spent the previous night with Mairi Chisolm.

The world is a very sad place – I have just been spending to-day busy up at N__ which is active, but mostly on our part, & last night with Mairi Chisholm at P – in the old cellarhouse where she is now – The Baroness was away & she was alone poor kiddy & very unhappy as the boy she had just got engaged to – young Jack Petre our cousin in the RN's – was killed 2 days ago in his machine in the Somme – They were only engaged privately so dont talk about it but I am so sorry for the poor little kid – she feels it dreadfully – all the more because she is a very quiet reserved little soul, as charming as the Baroness is 3rd-rate which is saying a lot – I am dreadfully sorry about it, he was such a nice boy & had a brilliant career – His machine came down like a stone through engine trouble while flying over the aerodrome & he was killed at once – He had been in the RNAS Squadron up here a long time.

Dorothie had also lost the man whom she had hoped to marry and, deep down, was still mourning his loss; she was able to give Mairi comfort and sympathy. She also asked her mother for a huge favour:

Mrs Ma dear I want to ask you to be a good Samaritan – Next time I come on leave may I suggest to Mairi Chisholm that if she can get away (which is rather doubtful) she should come to Newnham with me for 2 weeks? – She badly needs a complete change, she has not got a single member of her family to go & stay with & so wont go on leave – Jack Petries death she had felt dreadfully & it is so nice in May at N.P. it would do her good – She could share my room whenever you like & be no trouble – it would be sweet of you if I may suggest it her – Let me have an answer as soon as you get this, will you please?

[1 May 1917]

Peter did in fact get there. He 'blew in' and stayed for a few days and his visit followed the usual pattern:

> We have been pottering round & showing him the sights & all & to-night are having a binge in his honour at 14 & some of the sailors to dine – Great excitement because we have a tin of real cream a tin of raspberries & a tinned duck we have been saving up in case he came, so wont we all have tummy aches to-morrow morning my word – Tomorrow Prince Alexander has bidden me drag him to dine at the Mish – I can but hope he wont disgrace me by blowing bubbles in his soup.
>
> [19 April 1917]

Fortunately for Peter, he was not in Furnes when the Germans launched a terrible gas attack – he missed it by a day. There has also been 'a lot of activity' and Dorothie was waiting to find out what was going on before writing, but she needed to make sure her parents knew she had survived. The nauseating effect and horror of gas warfare is graphically described by Dorothie, who was lucky to escape serious harm.

> On 23rd about four a.m. Fritz suddenly started launching gas at us from the local metropolis up at N__ The wind wasnt very good for him too much to the N__ with the result the gas came diagonally back from the lines & we here at No. 14 got a very bad go of it – Jelly smelt it & woke up which was most intelligent of him – we all got up & threw on a few garments & of course hadnt a gas mask in the house as ours were on the car which that night happened to be in the other garage down in the town – There was the limousine here however & Jelly

started that & then he went off with the ambulance up to the lines & the gas being very bad by then I evacuated Winkie & Hélène & the family next door up to a hospital a few miles up the road – There I borrowed some gas masks & a spare driver as I was feeling rather faint & thought it best to have two drivers in the car – I left Winkie & Co there & tore back to No. 14 to find the gas had cleared away very quickly from there – as a matter of fact it had been following the road we took to the left & we were in it for 3 or 4 miles & so by bad luck got much more than the people who stayed here – By this time I was quite sure the Boche had over-run the sector as I couldn't imagine our having it so bad & the lines being still tenable – as a matter of fact the waves were very local – & came in gusts – For instance the main part of the town here got none – It just travelled down in long waves.

I rushed up to our barracks & was awfully relieved to find them all O.K. They had had very good masks & the main gas column had passed to the right of them & on our way.

Then we just worked like navvies all day till dark – simply never an engine stopped all day & we were all pretty beat up at the end of it – At the beginning Boche had rushed our lines but we drove them out again as the communiqué said & things are exactly as they were before now which is very satisfactory – The Sector was very lucky to get off with the line in the old place.

Its a dirty business gas & rather frightening – comes in great foggy waves & makes you cough your head off – Those poor poor devils of men – I cant tell you what its like to see them all lying about unconscious & in the most awful states – Much worse than blessés in a way because there is so desperately little you can do for them – In many cases they are all right for 12 to 24 hrs & then go down like logs – The Boche had a lot of casualties from our fire & we got some prisoners too.

I felt quite fairly allright the day itself after the 1st hour – just rather beat – It didn't work on me till 24 hrs after when at about 5 am I couldnt breathe except like a scared rabbit & went down to get a drink & then felt awfully faint – This kept coming on at intervals all that day, so I went to bed in the afternoon & have been there ever since – I am quite all right again now & getting up again now as I havent had a go of it since yesterday – Its a beastly feeling – You cant get a proper deep breath.

Winkie it affected quite differently – It made her cough awfully for 2 days – She is pretty right again too – Charles was awful fed up – He wheezed & was proper sorry for himself for several days – Jelly didn't feel it after the moment & all our people are OK. So would we have been if we had been able to get at our masks – All the Blokes party O.K. This is a long scrawl isnt it?

[26 April 1917]

Dorothie's extraordinary luck had saved her from permanent injury or possible death and the next time there was a gas alarm they were all ready for it – fortunately, that time it was a false one. The fighting continued.

Thérèse de Broqueville is staying with the Minister for a few days & came up to have supper with us – She had come to see Robert who is with his gun near Vimey, but he was recalled in a hurry & so she hardly saw him & was very depressed –

He seems to be have the most interesting time there – During the advance when their gun was being moved up again & he had nothing to do, he used to follow up behind the English infantry & amuse himself collecting Hun prisoners hiding in the dug-outs – He saw the English cavalry in action there at the beginning of the offensive – Apparently one of the reasons they lost so many was because the cavalry officers did not know the ground – Why they weren't acquainted with it thoroughly from o.p. etc. before the action I cant think.

The French are having an awfully stiff time of it down Rheims way owing to the Boche having chosen the same ground for a counter offensive – Had a short scrawl from Zettes Pa in the thick of it there – He says it is desperately hard fighting & a case of hand to hand fighting over every inch of ground to be won – Artillery preparation useless there as the Boche has so much massed too & counter shoots – Losses desperately heavy & things pretty stale mate on both sides – It's a pity & a waste of effort – I don't know what will be the next move now that had failed.

Poor France, she has been sadly 'éprouvée' [tested] in the war – Her losses compared to the population are overwhelming compared to ours. Down there in this offensive alone they have already had over 80,000 casualties. Of course the Boche must have lost a lot too, but not so many there as in front of the English – Peter writes they show no sign of moving them which is a good thing isn't it.

[4 May 1917]

At least Dorothie could get away from the war for a while and went home on leave on 17 May, taking Mairi and Winkie with her.

During her leave Dorothie became engaged to Captain Charles Moore. The Feildings and the Moores were part of the circle of Catholic families who knew each other well and mixed socially, and within which the sons and daughters sought a wife or husband. Charles's family had owned Mooresfort, an estate in Tipperary, since 1852, and his grandfather and father had served as MPs. His father, Arthur Moore, became a Catholic and was created a Count by Pope Leo XIII in 1879 and it may have been at this time that he became acquainted with the Feildings. The families were close and in 1877 Arthur married Mary Lucy Clifford, who was related to the Cliffords of Chudleigh, the family of Dorothie's mother. Charles, his second son, was born on 20 November 1880.

The two families had met frequently at social gatherings at their country estates before the war and Charles had stayed at Newnham Paddox for Christmas in 1912, 1913, and 1914. They had known each other a long time, and they had once become close, but at that time, as Dorothie explained later, their relationship was not satisfactory, so they returned to just being friends. However, during her leave things changed dramatically. Dorothie and Charles had spent ten days away at Newmarket and then visited Mooresfort – 'Such gorgeous weather – I am scribbling in the sun & the birds singing their hearts out & everything looking so perfect'. Dorothie had found the man she was looking for in 1914.

As their wedding was planned for early July, Dorothie returned to Flanders on 7 June, for the last time, 'to settle things a bit'. She told her father, 'It's so wonderful to feel perfect peace & happiness again, it seems almost another life since I have felt perfectly happy.' She had shed her sadness and in the days before she returned to Flanders seemed to have returned to being witty, light-hearted and her old self. Such a sudden change in her daughter may have upset the countess who was still mourning Hugh. In a letter to her mother Dorothie explained her change of heart with astonishing clarity:

Mother my darling – I got your sad letter last night & I have been a selfish beast – It seemed so wonderful to feel at peace & desire to live once more that I have you thinking all the help I have been to you these years is at an end – Mother dearest, my being happy won't come between us for 'a daughter is your daughter all her life' & our sympathy is too deep for anything to change it – At times I have wished I hadn't the power to feel things deeply & that the superficial beings are the happiest – But its not so – God gives you a bigger soul in exchange for pain & the power to be capable things –Sometime before the war Charles & I were very near caring for each other – Then, for no particular reason we drifted away imperceptibly back to just friendship – I think it was then I first began to think a good deal of Tom – Then Tom went to India & I never saw him again as I went straight to France – But we wrote to each other & in doing so had felt a deeper & newer affection growing out of our old camaraderie – We weren't engaged but I know we should have been had we met again – we both always thought we would meet again quite soon – Then he died just as my love was beginning to awaken & the bottom seemed to have fallen out of my life – I didn't care whether I lived or not so you see it wasn't very meritorious to be brave – I just threw myself heart &

soul into the work out here & I got to love my solders like my children – It was a positive need to me, to share the life & dangers of this war with them – My whole soul cried out for it & no other kind of work would have helped me one fraction as much; out here right at the heart & pulse of things one finds realities & greatness – The best of everyone comes out – But the sadness of it all worked its way into my very soul – of all those men who cared for me, it only made it harder & harder & the last 6 months I had got into a sort of mental stupor – I cant describe it – Just a great ache of loneliness – You see, God by teaching me suffering had given me a bigger soul capable of far deeper feeling, but had given me nothing else as yet to make up for the suffering.

I used to try & force myself sometimes to care for people I saw who sincerely loved & needed me, so that I might make them happy – But then at the last minute there was never anything but bare friendship & it couldnt suffice me & I was afraid to marry with only that.

When I met Charles the other day & he told me how he cared, I felt for the 1st time that he could awaken my power to love (which I thought had died in me) if he loved me strongly & enough – At the very beginning I was afraid perhaps my loneliness was influencing me unduly & that I had not yet found the real thing – But so very soon I was quite, quite sure everything was right – The big things in Charles had not been stirred before the war – He was inclined to be idle & drift through life without being properly alive – The army & war generally has done to him what it has done to many people including myself – He loves me so much, Mother dearest, & so deeply that he has made me love him; it is not just a wild wave of sentimentality, it is a real thing which grows greater every day & is coupled with an infinite trust & confidence in him & in what the future will bring – Please God, he will be some months at home, before all the mental 'angoisse' begins again – I am feeling so small & stormtossed, I couldnt bear any more just yet – I just need a little bit of peace & happiness so badly Mother dearest – I could keep going before without it Mother darling – Now I seem just to crumple up & I couldn't stand anymore just for a while.

[12 June]

It was again owing to Dorothie's astonishing luck that Charles had proposed at this time. She had told her mother that she was glad that she had come back at that time as there were going to be changes. The British objective was to clear the Belgian coast of Germans, partly to eliminate the U-boat bases at Ostend and Zeebrugge and partly to allow an outflanking of German defences in Belgium. The Belgians were desperately short of men and ammunition and by this time were running out of financial resources. The plan was that the Belgians stepped aside and allowed the British to take over the Front at Nieuwpoort. Plans were also being made for a huge offensive, which became known as the Third Battle of the Ypres, or more familiarly as Passchendaele.

Dorothie knew that matters would be run differently and that the Munro Ambulance Corps and her job there would no longer be required. Everything was to be run by the British and put on a much more formal basis. The Belgians had allowed Dorothie a great deal of freedom as a woman at the Front, but even then, she was aware that it was wiser to behave discreetly. 'Whenever gens change I keep awfully quiet & hide when I see them till they get accustomed to me being here, in case they said "Hell! a woman" – & get excited at my being here.' The British were going to be far more rigorous; all her charm and connections were not going to soften their resolve. There would be no place in Flanders for Dorothie, she would have to find an alternative occupation and no longer be at the 'heart and pulse of things'. What better alternative could she be offered? Great happiness and a peaceful future with the man she loved.

LIFE AFTER FLANDERS

Dorothie and Charles married on 5 July 1917 in the Catholic Chapel at Newnham Paddox and among the guests were recuperating soldiers who had not yet returned to the Front. (See p. 223.) After the wedding, the Moores went on honeymoon to Ireland, where Charles drove them round, calling on friends and staying in Killarney. They visited Mooresfort for a few days, then left for Dublin. During her honeymoon Dorothie continued to write to her mother. She described the country as 'almost just too beautiful' and the most lovely 'purple' evenings reminded her of her visit to Granada in 1909. She and Charles were obviously very happy, and her letters are full of her usual humour: 'The car is great fun but we are now running out of petrol & will I expect have to go to Mooresfort by train – But who cares, it's not ours so we can leave it in a ditch somewhere.'

However, her happiness did not stop her thinking about her friends in Nieuwpoort where the Germans had finally

Wedding portrait,
1917, by Anglo-
Hungarian painter
Philip de László, many
of his sitters royalty
and aristocrats.

reached the locks. 'I am most awfully distressed to see the bad
communiqué ... I hope all my friends are ok & the sailors &
all, but it's beastly & I can't get it out of my head.' She was
also trying to get news of Peter, whom she had missed when he
was on leave and had planned to meet in London.

Owing to Charles's army connections, Dorothie was
informed in great detail about what was happening in
Flanders:

Ladies Imperial Club, Dover Street, Piccadilly, W1 1st Aug.
Mother dear
We have been trying to get news of Peter's whereabouts for
you & Squeaks & Charles has seen divers people, one just back.
The rumour that they were at Nieupoort is wrong. The guards

What was left of Nieuwpoort in 1917.

attacked directly opposite Boesenjhe, marching on the right of the French. The latter had very light casualties. Guards casualties unknown as yet – Irish G's were in the 1st attacking bit. The Guards were divided into 3 Brigades for the stunt to go on in turn. Peter's was the third to go if needed. So that means his people only went if badly needed which is unlikely & Da tells P. was down to stay back as 2nd in com for the 1st shove, so I think this this will make you less anxious ... Just dining with Da & then back home ... I am praying hard you may not have too much anxiety over Peter these days but so far it has been so lucky the way everything has turned out.

Dorothie was also worried about Charles's health. Under the stress of the excitement of his marriage to Dorothie, added to the strain of war, Charles had contracted pleurisy:

(Mixed feelings) 3rd August

Charles was vetted yesterday in London by his doctor who says that there is still a certain amount of adhesion after his pleurisy – He still feels it you know at times – The Dr. says he wouldnt consider him fit for a board for about 2 months as until it has cleared off entirely exposure or a bad chill would

Image of the first Battle of Passchendaele by photographer Frank Hurley. It is a composite image, one of four versions with different 'sunburst' formations in the clouds created from separate negatives. 'A terrible beauty is born.'

This image was originally captioned: 'A street corner in Poelcappelle, Belgium'.

go to the lungs again – He has to go for a regular board again with the Dr's chit & so I hope it will mean he is here for about 2 months for sure yet – Of course if they should be hard up for officers after this push he would go & chance it.

Still thank goodness for adhesions & long may it adhere!

There was still no news of Peter.

In Flanders the Third Battle of Ypres, Passchendaele, had been launched on 31 July 1917 and continued until the fall of Passchendaele village on 6 November. Although there was no news of Peter, news of deaths filtered through and on 5 August Dorothie wrote to her mother, eager to comfort her; but she also needed to share the loss of Charles's friends with her mother.

> ... I wired you Charles went up to London to see the orderly room & they said Peter was alright as they had the unofficial list of casualties & no mention of him. The Irish Guards have lost a good lot of officers. They led you know. Poor Charles is awfully low because his 3 best friends were all killed that day. Col Eric Greer (married Pam Fitzgerald) Sir John Dyer and Father Knaps who was to have married us. All 3 were with him all the while in France & are about the only ones of his old lot still out there.

Charles was 'low' owing to the shock and despair at the death of almost 250 officers of the 2nd Battalion Irish Guards. Both he and Dorothie knew life had to continue nonetheless, and visits were made to Ireland to socialise, and for Charles to check on the horses and farm at Mooresfort:

> 28 September 1917
> Friday
> Had enjoyed myself at the Curragh. Enjoyed myself disgustingly – our 2 little nags ran awfully well. Sister Barvey won her Race but was dead-heated by another gee owing to her fool jockey making a mistake – But that was good anyway, then Judsea the nag we put all our hopes on was a close second in the big race at the Turf Club Cup – Both were bred at Mooresfort – I go so excited I nearly burst & am all of a dither still.

News of Peter came at last. Despite the hopes and prayers of his family, and the optimism of his sister Dorothie, Peter had been wounded in action near Broembeek, Belgium, on 9 October, and died just after midnight on 11 October, aged 23. He was buried at Dozinghem Military Cemetery.

His commanding officer, General Follett, wrote to the earl:

I cannot tell you what a loss he is both as a friend and a soldier. It was the first time that he commanded a company in action, and he was doing so well. He was full of enthusiasm for this attack and I only wish he could have seen the successful ending of such a great day for the regiment, but all the officers of his company fell wounded before reaching the final objective.

Devastated, the countess decided to close Newnham as a hospital and move to London. Dorothie wrote to comfort her:

I know so well how absolutely down & out you are – Thank God the hospital is closing & it won't be so hard in London away from the dreadful memories of Newnham – Mother dearest I would so willingly have given myself to keep one of your two dear lads – But God did not seem to will it so – The poor mothers have so much, so much more to bear than anyone else these dreadful days.

[12 October 1917]

Meanwhile, Charles recovered enough to rejoin his regiment and returned to France. Dorothie was dismayed and wrote to her mother, 'I had been so afraid of this these

last days – oh Mother darling pray hard – I am so afraid.'
Still mourning Peter, this was an extremely anxious time for
Dorothie and her worst fears were realised when Charles
was wounded on 17 April 1918. He had been shot but
fortunately only in the thigh, which left him with a limp.
He was shipped back to recover in a London hospital and
did not return to the Front. In September he was awarded
the Military Cross:

Capt. C J Moore – Irish Guards

In a situation of extreme gravity, when the troops on their right
had been forced out of their trenches by the intensity of the fire,
this officer collected them, loading them back through a heavy
barrage to the original line, when he stayed with them, walking
down the line under sniping & machine gun fire until their
confidence had returned.

His courage and coolness were an example to all.

[*London Gazette* 16 September]

Whilst Charles was still serving with the Irish Guards, he and
Dorothie made their home in Surrey at the Irish Guards HQ
at Pirbright Barracks in Coulsden. Their London home was
Warley Mount, Brentwood, until 1922 when Charles resigned
his commission. Dorothie's personality had not altered with
her happiness: she still needed to do something useful, so
until the end of the war she drove ambulances for the London
Military Hospital. 'I am busy driving Fido Fiat & like the work
very much – lots to do & one feels refreshingly useful again –
I had got tired of being merely ornamental.' In in her free time,
she visited family and friends around the country and hunted

LADY DOROTHIE MOORE
Will give TWO
HUNT PARTIES
with THEATRICALS at
MOORESFORT, near TIPPERARY
— ON —
Friday, 4th January
(In aid of the Scarteen Black and-Tan Hunt Funds). 1935.

AFTERNOON PARTY---3-30 to 7-30.
Tickets 5/- each, inclusive of Tea. (Children half price).
THEATRICALS, followed by Tea, Bridge and Dancing.

EVENING PARTY---9 p.m.
Tickets 2/6 each, inclusive of Buffet Refreshments. (No Reduction for Children)
THEATRICALS, followed by Whist, Bridge, "45" & Roulette.

All Tickets can be had from LADY DOROTHY MOORE, Mooresfort, Tipperary, or at the door. Please apply beforehand whenever possible.

McKern's, Printers.   MOORESFORT IS 1 MILE FROM LATTIN.

Above: Marquis Hubert Octave Ganay Behague on St. Martin, Celia on Thuby, Dorothie on Alberic, 1931.

Left: Poster for Dorothie's fundraising activities.

in the winter months at home with the Atherstone Hunt, the local pack she had hunted with since childhood.

The war ended on 11 November 1918 and for many this was of course worthy of celebration; but not for Dorothie. She told her mother:

I couldn't bear to hear the people laughing & clapping yesterday – One was so haunted by the memories of those dear boys who have gone – But Mother dear thank God that supreme sacrifice was not for nothing as I have often feared it would be.

In 1919, Dorothie and Charles were delighted by the prospect of their first child, but her mother died three days before the birth. Dorothie must have been distraught and the baby's birth on 8 December a mixture of joy and grief. The family believed that the countess had worn herself out in the running of her home as a hospital and, added to the loss of her two sons in the Great War, her health broke down. She died, it was said, of a broken heart.

A second daughter was born to the Moores in 1920 in a Rugby nursing home. This birth was traumatic because the birth was breech and Dorothie was very ill afterwards. She wrote to Charles and it is clear that she thought she was going to die, asking Charles 'not to grieve for me if I should leave you now'. She must have been remembering the losses of her two brothers and her mother.

However, Dorothie's love and appreciation of the beautiful things in life was never far away. As she was lying in the nursing home, she told Charles that 'the last notes of a blackbird's goodnight song have just come into my room to fill me with contentment and with peace.' She recovered and returned to Pirbright, Charles and her new baby. Two more daughters were born and in 1925, Dorothie and Charles took their family to live at Mooresfort.

After the First World War, Ireland was split from 1919–1921 by the Irish War of Independence, fought between Irish separatists (organised as the Irish Republic) and the British government. This was then followed by the Irish Civil War from June 1922 until May 1923, so it was considered not safe to take a family to Ireland – travelling by car or train would be courting danger. However, the Moores were much respected and loved as landowners and employers and this is probably why Charles was safe and the house never damaged. Charles's father, Arthur Moore, had been well known and respected as a good Irish Catholic who had given generously to the church and built Roscrea Abbey, and this may be the reason why Mooresfort was one of the few great houses in Ireland during this period that was not burned to the ground. Charles occasionally went to deal with estate business but did not stay long, leaving the running of Mooresfort to his farm manager.

For the next nine years family life followed a pattern similar to that before the Great War. Dorothie ran the house with the help of servants and the governess was the daughter of one of Dorothie's Belgian friends. The children's lives were typical of a wealthy aristocratic family. Their mother had experienced a very happy childhood, blessed with adoring parents and enjoying good relationships with all her siblings. She was determined that her children should enjoy the same good fortune. In 1928, the birth of their son brought great joy and excitement for the family, their friends and all the servants. The children were taught the sense of duty and high principles that their class owed to their country and all levels of society, to serve and respect everyone, especially servants. Dorothie reprimanded one of her daughters for cheeking a servant. 'You must never be rude to people who are not in a position to answer back.'

Mooresfort was frequently full of visitors and Dorothie and Charles were often away on return visits. Sometimes they took the children and there are memories of 'wonderful, lazy afternoons boating on the lake' at Rudyard Kipling's estate at Batemans. The children stayed at home or with relatives in England whilst their parents visited France, Belgium and

Bateman's, Rudyard Kipling's home in Burwash, is now a public museum dedicated to the author.

Italy and Dorothie kept up a lively correspondence with them. Charles's duties as papal count required him to attend the pope for one month a year, and he was in Rome in March 1929. Dorothie, accompanied by her sister Mollie and her husband, went to visit him.

> Wed. 20th March
>
> Sea as flat as a table. France was brown & ugly from snow. Italy is greener but not so green as Ireland. Sun and blue sky. Wanted to send a flower in the envelope but feared it will be dried out. It is now all soft and fluffy like Bingo & smells delicious.

Dorothie promised to bring the children some Italian soap. 'Sending stamps – couldn't get song books, out of print, but got story books instead. Busy praying this holy week – lovely music in all the churches.'

She enclosed a picture of the Pope, Pius XI,

> '... to take to Billy Halligan, [one of their farm hands], to bless him as he has been hurt. The Holy Father sends a special blessing to everyone at Mooresfort ... We spent half-an-hour in the Pope's private room with Cecil and Mollie.

Just as Dorothie and her siblings had done, the Moore children gave parties in the drawing room and Dorothie filled it with wild flowers, especially daisies and primroses. The local children were invited to see plays and charades which had been written by the family, dressed in costumes they had made. Tea followed these entertainments, then each child visitor received a present. The Moores were known as generous and kind;

Dorothie treated all children just like her own children and made sure that they had a good time.

When not travelling, Dorothie was involved with all the usual country activities, one of which was the local Agricultural Society. Charles owed a stud that cared for King George V's yearlings, and both Dorothie and Charles attended race meetings. Dorothie had always been a keen huntswoman and she joined the Scarteen Hunt and became a regular feature at hunt meets. In 1935 the *Irish Times* reported that she had been 'prominently associated with the Scarteen Hunt to the success of which her great organising powers in no small degree contributed'. Dorothie was considered to be an excellent and proficient rider, always riding side-saddle, and it was agreed by everyone who knew about horses that she had a perfect 'seat' and always looked immaculate in her hunting clothes. Every morning she arranged for a bunch of Parma violets that had been grown in the greenhouse to be made up and worn by herself and each visitor who hunted that day.

One of the estate workers recalled his father eulogising about Dorothie. He remembered her as being a real 'lady' in the true sense of the word and also her kindness and generosity to his own family. He recalled her riding side-saddle in the local hunts and he said there wasn't a ditch or a dyke in Tipperary that would 'best' her, and 'You'd stand in snow to watch her handle a horse.'

Dorothie had not lost her adventurous spirit and still took calculated risks. One winter's day Charles was driving his Rolls-Royce down a country road when he became aware of galloping hooves on the road behind. He parked the car near a hedge and got out to remonstrate with the rider – galloping on tarmac is bad for the horses and was just not done. He was amazed to identify the rider as his wife! She must have also recognised her husband and knew he would be furious. She did not stop, came straight at the car and lifted the horse, soaring over both car and the hedge, and galloped off into the distance, leaving Charles stunned. She hoped by the time she arrived home he would have calmed down.

The family tradition of kind acts, religious piety and help for the sick was followed by the Moores. Billy Halligan, to whom Dorothie sent a card from the pope, worked on the estate in the 1920s and early 1930s. He became ill and was sent to London for diagnosis paid for by Charles. It was cancer and there was no hope. Back at home Dorothie and Charles visited him and brought food, especially bowls of soup. (These may have brought back memories of those days in Flanders when she and her companions made vast pots of soup for the soldiers in the trenches.) The family prayed for him at Mass and drew a cross on the door and when he died Dorothie discreetly helped his family by giving the children money for opening gates when the hunt passed through. Dorothie was subtle – an act of charity was disguised as a small wage for performing a useful task.

Although Charles and Dorothie never spoke of the Great War, they were very much aware of the damage and distress caused to the local families. Dorothie became an active member of the British Legion in Tipperary, which was providing help for the numerous ex-service men and women who had returned to live in their hometowns. She organised fundraising events and visited the veterans and their families, particularly those who had lost family members. Every summer Dorothie held a garden party and organised a bus to bring her guests to Mooresfort where they were given a meal, after which they were entertained by a local band. On other occasions, guests were entertained by a celebrated singer, Count McCormack, the famous Irish tenor, who regularly came to sing. In 1914 he had been the first singer to record *It's a long, long way to Tipperary*, which may have stirred memories for his listeners at Mooresfort. There was also a singer in the Feilding family. Dorothie's aunt Winifride had married Gervase Elwes, a famous and distinguished tenor. Dorothie had played recordings of him during her days

John Francis McCormack, Irish lyric tenor and Papal Count.

in Flanders and found his songs very moving. She no doubt persuaded him to entertain her guests when he and her aunt visited Mooresfort.

It must have seemed to Dorothie and Charles that after their traumatic experiences in the Great War and the the loss of dearly loved family and friends, their life now was idyllic. It is therefore ironic that, after the many close escapes from death and injury during the war, followed by sixteen years of happiness, at the age of forty-five Dorothie's luck finally deserted her; tragedy was about to blight the lives of the Moore family. It was Billie Halligan's son, Johnny, who remembered clearly after eighty years an accident that may throw light on Dorothie's death. She was out hunting, was thrown, and the horse fell on top of her. Dorothie had not returned at the usual time and Charles was frantic with worry as he had no idea where she was. Then news came of the accident, and it was said that she was found unconscious. She recovered but Johnny commented that after that, 'she wasn't the same anymore and got more and more ill'. He described her complexion as 'yellow and less glowing'.

The accident may have happened in the hunting season of 1933/34. Her health declined and she became noticeably ill at the beginning of 1935. By April she was aware that she was seriously ill.

April 27 1935
My dearest Husband
I have nothing to add to what I wrote all those years ago at the Rugby Nursing Home, for I find I love you just as much.

You have been so sweet to me during this long illness, that if I die in the near future it will be without fear or regrets. Life to me is like a flame & I would rather mine were blown out than see it gutter out. We have such happy memories behind us. I hope still we may live to see our children old enough to start upon their individual lives – but that must depend upon the will of God.

    ... God bless you my darling man and all my sweet children. Put your big arms round me & I will fear nothing – all I need is your love and you have all of mine.

Your devoted wife

During the summer of 1935 her bed was brought down and put in the drawing room, where she could see her beloved Galtee Mountains in the distance. A nursing nun was in constant attendance, and doctors visited twice a week. It is possible that the fall had damaged her internal organs, particularly her liver, hence the jaundice colour, and infection may have set in. With no antibiotics, there was no cure. Her illness may also have been exacerbated by her experiences in the Great War when she was exposed to gas.

In the autumn she was taken back upstairs and on the evening of 24 October Charles took the children aside and told them quietly that their mother had died.

To be given to my children – at my death
May 6 1935
If I leave you soon I do not wish you to grieve – for I love you too dearly one & all. Just think of me standing on the bank, waving goodbye to you all as you set off on the spring

tide of the river of life, each paddling your own canoe. Because, remember, no one else will paddle it half as well as you do yourself provided you put your heart & soul into the undertaking & don't expect anyone else to do everything for you – you have all been brought up to be independent – Real happiness comes from inner contentment of the soul & an appreciation of all the beautiful and amusing things that abound in our daily lives provided we use the senses that God gave us. So don't let me overhear St. Peter whispering that he has overheard any child of mine say he or she has been 'dogged with bad luck all my life' – your 'luck' is not just a question of money – If you have what is necessary to keep real anxiety away then you are lucky & and have nothing very serious to complain of.

Your characters are formed enough already for me to know that you should all be able to face such difficulties as are likely to come your way.

Your father's devotion to you all & his appreciation of nice things will I know always keep you good friends both with him & with each other. So dear creatures I give you all the biggest hug that ever was. Don't wear mourning but think kindly of me in your hearts.

Yr loving mother

Two days later her coffin was taken down the mile-long drive – the two youngest children walked behind it to the gates, accompanied by the estate workers and house staff. Then Dorothie took her last journey back to Newnham Paddox where she was buried in the family cemetery by the Catholic Chapel on 27 October 1935. Thirteen months later her brother

Rollo also died, his wife Mellins following him after only a few weeks. Rollo was buried next to Dorothie. Her father, having lost his beloved Dodo, his three sons, and two months into another war, died in November 1939 and was buried the other side of his daughter. Charles lived on until 1962 and was buried at Roscrea, the monastery near Tipperary that had been built by his grandfather.

For decades, very few people spoke about the Great War. Certainly, Dorothie and Charles never discussed their experiences and losses and when Charles was asked years later, he said it was too painful. Nevertheless, the memories were there, deeply buried. For Dorothie, writing had often provided

Mount St Joseph Abbey, Roscrea, Tipperary, where Charles is buried.

the opportunity to express fears and emotions, as well as to make observations on what she saw around her. It seems appropriate that in a book in which Dorothie's words have so often revealed her true self, we should end with her own writing. Let us remember the courage, sacrifice and empathy of Lady Dorothie Feilding, a decorated and much-loved heroine, during the war in Flanders from 1914 to 1917.

It is my birthday and whilst I was writing at my desk this morning, I heard the door open softly & the approach of hesitating footsteps – A moment later a shaking hand laid a lovely old cameo brooch on my table. I looked up & saw Johanna, the old house-keeper and friend of the family – My children belong to the fifth generation she has seen under this roof.

'I'd like to see you wear it – It is a relic', she says, pushing the brooch towards me.

Seldom has a gift touched me more, for I know the value she sets upon it. The setting has become friendly and warm with the handling of many years & is made of charming old fashioned twisted gold work.

The background of the brooch is of apricot coloured alabaster that awakens memories of the sun kissed columns of the Acropolis, glowing in the golden light of an Athenian evening.

The cameo itself is of the delicately carved profile of an angel of pity.

It is near midnight now & the house is quiet & still as I sit by the flickering firelight – My thoughts go back to a day in the autumn of 1914 when the war and many of us were young. I was one of a motley company of voluntary ambulance drivers in Flanders then. We had a convoy consisting of every known variety of car. There were a few ambulances, two ancient chain driven converted shooting brakes from a Scottish moor, several requisitioned limousines, a taxi and a grey low-hung open Rolls-Royce.

Still, God knows we were thankful enough for small mercies and willing slaves those cars proved. The battle line in the north had become more or less of a fixture at last; the weeks of disorder and despair of armies in retreat was over.

That day in particular had been a long and tiring one. We were endeavouring to help stem the stream of the wounded of three nations and the roads were shell pocked & a welter of mud & debris.

In one village we had seen two weary French soldiers sit down on the pavement with their backs to a wall, whilst they ate some food they had been lucky enough to collect.

A rather larger shell than usual burst close to them – As the smoke cleared we were relieved to find the men had not altered their position – The elder was still leaning against the wall with his food in his hand and the younger solder was huddled up against his comrade. We went over to them – There was no sign of fear on either of their faces, nor had the shell made any mark upon them.

Both men were dead.

That night my car amongst others was sent to the outskirts of Nieuport Bains to wait for stretcher bearers who were collecting the wounded from an exposed part of the line. The village in question had been under fire all day but as ammunition was scarce on both sides, the gunners were only too thankful to leave well alone.

The previous August that little village had been a prosperous seaside tripper resort – Jaunty villas with gay coloured roofs and shutters had been hives of busy pleasure-seeking humanity. Now the houses were burning one by one in the still night air.

Curling tongues of flame went creeping from building to building, devouring all before them. Now & then towering pillars of flame were preceded by dull thuds as ceilings & roofs fell in. It reminded me of the scene in 'Valkyrie' where the flames encircle Brünhilde's bier. In this case the lovely roll & thunder of the surf upon the beach was the only orchestra.

I lay back, weary in body with my mind full of bitter thoughts of the hideousness and futility of war. Away above my head curled a great bank of sand, tufted with sea grasses so that it looked like the crest of a gigantic wave about to break. The dunes on all sides were pearly white and eerie in the radiance of a forgiving moon.

In the distance the desultory crack of rifle fire alternated with the merciless toc-toc of the machine guns. At intervals a spent bullet would bury itself somewhere in the sand with a 'phut'. All feeling of time had ceased to exist, when out of one of the cellars of a ruined house, the liquid notes of a beautiful tenor voice began to stream out into the night.

The singer was a Zouave soldier, until a few weeks before attached to the Marseilles opera house. The song was the clown's song from 'Pagliaci'. That wonderful melody that contains all the tragedies and sorrows of the world. Listening in the moonlight, I felt it was more beauty than I could bear just then.

The song ended with that haunting break in the clown's voice. To me it was the lament of all those unhappy women whose men were and are not.

Yes, old Johanna was right – It is well to remember, lest we forget.

EXAMPLES OF DOROTHIE'S LETTERS

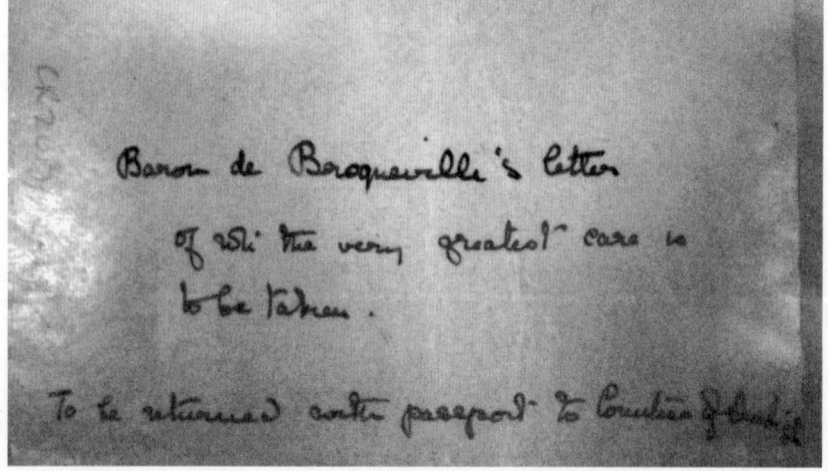

Jan⁶⁰

Mother o Squeaks –

I got your note at
supper on New Years day, I was
just delighted – That is
grand – Come on the 14ᵗʰ please
as that is the day suits Broqueville
best – Do as follows for jolly trip

1 – Get your passports & have them
viséd to cross via Boulogne or
Calais – The latter closest but
boats don't always run.

2 – Broqueville will instruct Com–

CR 7002/ 1552/1

MUNRO AMBULANCE CORPS,
ARMY POST OFFICE, S.10,
B.E.F.

Jan 6&

Mother dear :

I got your letter & the one to
Broq. last night & have sent it on to
him — You ask me to be sure & settle
whether to meet you Calais a Boulogne?
But the situation is this —

There is on a daily service from
Folkestone to both places —

But whenever mines or sub
troubles a scares, one service is liable
at any moment to be cancelled for a
few days, & as often as not there is
no way of finding out until one actually

(18801/6582/6)

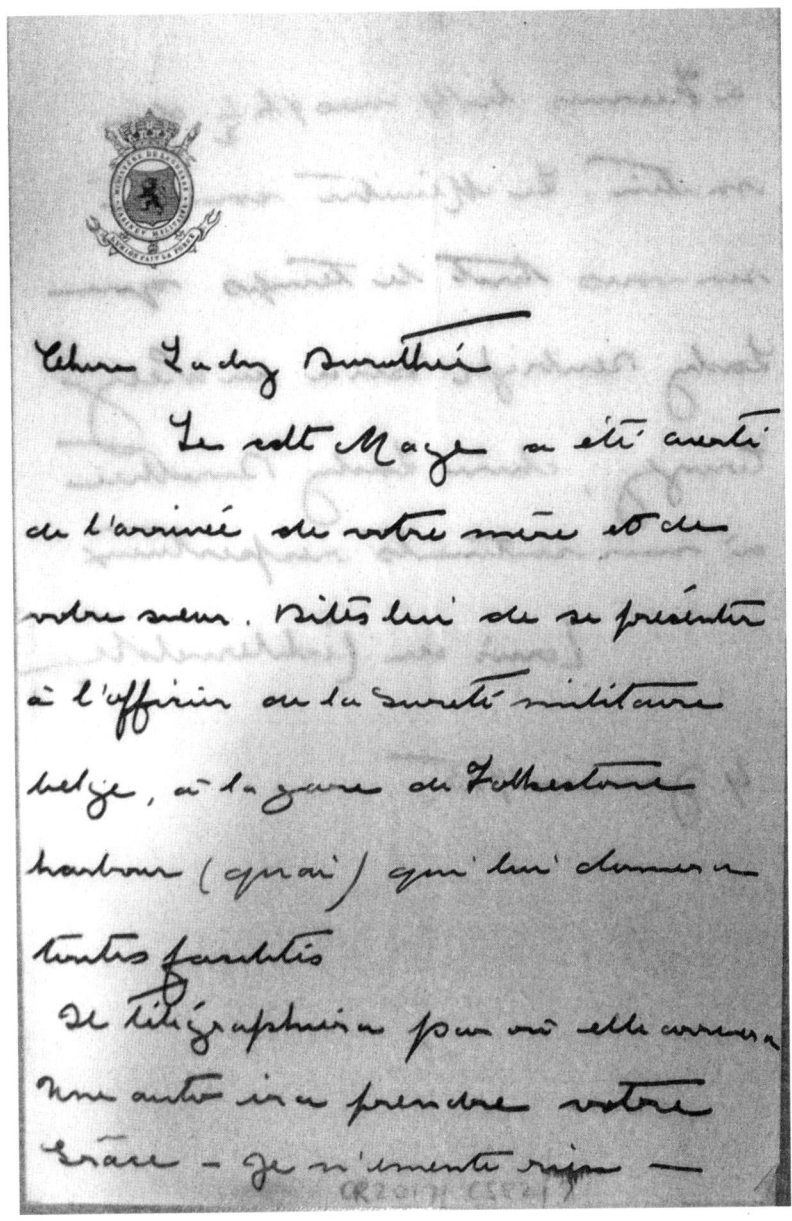

— La jeune et jolie infirmière: « Maintenant,
Général , regardez où vous voudrez, mais pas
en l'air, s'il vous plaît ... »
— Le Général : " Soyez tranquille, Mademoiselle." —

— La jeune
« jolie infirmière : " Je crois qu'il
vaut mieux que je me mette le dos au
soleil ".
— Le général : " . . . . "

Dorothie, Dr Jellett and Charles in Nieuwpoort; drawing by General Hély d'Oissel.

POEMS WRITTEN BY DOROTHIE

The Attack

Headquarters say
The crest must be ours,
Before many hours,
Cost what it will.

Crash follows crash,
The guns are speaking.
Whistling and shrieking
The shells drive by.

Darkness is torn
By great sheets of flame.
Horror without name
Shadows the earth.

Amidst the foe
Death still sows the seed
Of her might and greed
In flesh and blood.

The English wait
Half stunned by the noise.
Crouching they are poised
So tense and still.

Dawn is at hand,
The sky is aglow.
Grey mist hanging low
Half shrouds the fields.

Up as one man
That dull khaki wave
Of men strong and brave
Pour to attack.

The National Review

Two hundred yards
Of bare open ground.
With hardly a sound
Limply they fall.

As bullets hiss by
The ranks are thinning.
Bayonets glinting
Still they push on.

All is over –
Achieved is the goal.
War has taken her toll,
But triumph is theirs.

The new-born day
Breaks o'er the hill-side,
Red, after the tide
Of battle past.

Beyond the sea
The womenfolk – wait,
Since all time their fate
Hardest of all.

INDEX

Also available from Amberley Publishing

FEATURED IN THE *NEW YORK POST*
AND *THE DAILY TELEGRAPH*

HER FINEST HOUR
THE HEROIC LIFE OF DIANA ROWDEN, WARTIME SECRET AGENT

GABRIELLE McDONALD-ROTHWELL

Also available from Amberley Publishing

BRITAIN'S **A** HERITAGE

Women in the
Second World War

Neil R. Storey & Fiona Kay